NEAR THE FAR BAMBOO

Near the Far Bamboo

*An insightful look at cross-cultural clashes
through the eyes of a tentmaking missionary*

Martin St. Kilda

CHRISTIAN PUBLICATIONS
CAMP HILL, PENNSYLVANIA

Christian Publications
3825 Hartzdale Drive, Camp Hill, PA 17011

The mark of  vibrant faith

ISBN: 0-87509-510-0
LOC Catalog Card Number: 93-70739
© 1993 by Wade F. Bradshaw
All rights reserved
Printed in the United States of America

93 94 95 96 97 5 4 3 2 1

Cover illustration by Ron Wheeler

Dedication:

*With grateful appreciation, these thoughts are
dedicated to **Hermon Paul Pressler III**, a faithful
recruiting agent of the kingdom of God.*

CONTENTS

How Dare You, of All People, Write This Book!

I was asked once by the pastor of our village church to preach the sermon the following week. He did not call it "preaching," however, because it was against the law to preach in that Hindu nation. So instead, I was invited to "share" with the little congregation.

A friend in the mission, equipped with his Master of Divinity degree from a prestigious school of theology, turned to me in surprise, saying that he had not realized that I had been to seminary. I replied that I had never studied theology but that I had been listening to sermons on something near a weekly basis for the past thirty years and that, after all, should count for something.

This book is written hesitantly, after one brief, three-year term in the country of Dhurgastan. Compared with other missionaries who have invested long careers of faithful obscurity in that unusual place, I deserve no one's attention, and even less admiration than attention. On the other hand, I do have one odd attribute to commend me: I have been a Christian missionary for a short time after having been a layman for a much longer time.

Whatever else that may mean, it allows me to lay claim to some knowledge of missions and yet be able to recall the strange impressions left by the rumpled missionaries that visited our church. I can remember what it is like to be obtuse in geography or to know all of the arguments against communism without ever having met a communist. All of my previous knowledge of Islam and Buddhism came from books with titles like *Know Their Weaknesses*. Slide presentations of malnourished children and statistics on world population left me frustrated. Does this mean that we should cancel lunch with our friends at the cafeteria after the sermon? Is it wicked to want children of my own when we could be adopting Koreans?

The gap between foreign missionaries and those who send them is greater than it needs to be. Narrowing that distance is not unlike translation work. A foreign student approaches you and, without giving any context, asks for a definition of the English word "quarter." Initially it seems a simple proposition. There is the mathematical usage of four equal parts. And then there is the United States coin . . . or maybe he meant the term as used by accountants or, perhaps in football. Hmmm . . . more complicated than it seemed, you turn in your collegiate dictionary and find seventeen different definitions. Everything from part of a horse's foot to the mercy extended to vanquished foes.

Simply defining the work of missions turns out to have nothing simple about it; there are different faces under different circumstances. Church planting to new cropping systems is included, and the field grows wider as an attempt is made to address the modern world's complexity. The people making that attempt, however, are not as different from one's next door neighbor as the layman would like to believe.

As I write, I can do so as an authority on only my own experiences; and I suppose that I could even misinterpret those.

An author does best to stay with the time-tested format of chronological order. But even this method has its confusion, causing a reader to run up and down through the years in order to understand a particular motive or friendship. The alternative is to write topically, but here each subject hangs as a separate beach towel out to dry. My method includes both; I trust it will be easy to follow.

I use as my sources monthly prayer letters written en masse to our list of supporters, my journal (which I kept with varying degrees of success) and excerpts from the letters written to my parents every Saturday afternoon (with little variation). Home on furlough, I supplement these with my reflections on the time spent there. Dhurgastan grows both more vague and in focus when held at arm's length.

Martin St. Kilda

The Nation of Dhurgastan

Area: 125,000 square kilometers, a mountain-ringed Himalayan state bordering India, China and Nepal.

Population: 11 million, annual growth is a very rapid 2.8%; literacy—men, 22%; women, 12%; there are over 60 different tribes and people groups; Basha is the major language among 51 dialects.

Capital: Rajdhani, 250,000 inhabitants, urbanization of the country, 4%.

Economy: The world's second poorest nation according to United Nations' figures, a largely undeveloped economy with few manufactured products, almost totally reliant in trade upon India. Transportation is very limited in this mountainous land.

Politics: Nonaligned dictatorship with a popularly elected, partiless parliament.

Religion: Hinduism and Buddhism are often blended, 96%; Muslims, 3%, primarily along the border with India; Christians, 15,000 known believers. Christian missions are tolerated as long as they do not seek converts. Proselytizing carries a 6-year prison sentence. Those convicted of changing their religion may be imprisoned for 3 years.

CHAPTER 1
_____

His Hand in Hindsight

The Call of God

"They are perfectly right in believing that God allows nothing to remain unordered and that He knows all things before they come to pass. He is the Cause of all causes, although not of all choices."

St. Augustine

No question is more commonly asked of a foreign missionary. It is asked by the mission board at the initial interviews, by supporters periodically and by colleagues on fellowship evenings. "How did you experience God's call to serve as a missionary?" Perhaps it is significant that the people one goes to live and labor among are the only ones to never ask it.

Though commonly asked, it remains a sticky one to answer; there is a temptation to develop, once and for all, a glib answer. Something with just the right combination of humility and whizbang circumstances to leave a favorable impression. One's answer may even change and evolve over time, which is a strange thing considering the idea that God's call is a one time, unmistakable event like the birth of a nephew. It must either have happened or else it did not.

The slightest hesitation in answering the question—anything other than an immediate, confident answer—and the friendly expression can be seen to drain from the questioner's face. Just keep it simple, please; nothing messy and complicated, thank you. God calls. You pick up the receiver and listen; after that you proceed to a travel agent and purchase your ticket to Outer Mimbwebwe.

This simple, harmless question is a very real tension for some missionaries. I know plenty of talented, eloquent people ministering overseas who would much prefer to face the spears of ten thousand warlike pagans than a small, nodding missions committee armed with good intentions and that one innocent question.

Do not misunderstand. God can and does call His servants; only often it is not the neat, orderly, tersely worded telex that others expect to hear about.

> To: Martin St. Kilda
> From: Heaven. Personnel Department, Foreign Service
> Re: New Assignment
>
> PROCEED AT ONCE TO NEAREST MISSION
> AGENCY STOP LEAVE ALL POSSESSIONS STOP
> GO TO MIMBWEBWE AND TRANSLATE SCRIPTURES
> INTO UNKNOWN LANGUAGE STOP
> SOLI DEO GLORIA

One does hear of those who receive the required call, a vision, an unshakable compulsion, an incredible alignment of unusual circumstances; but many make the decision with no more light than when they chose between mechanical and electrical engineering back in college. The world's needs, our desires, gifts and talents, useful opportunities, the counsel of those with our best interests at heart all act to make the decision and to muddy the waters. The call of God sediments into that same tension faced by every Christian sooner or later: I want to please God, but what is His will in this specific situation?

A person prays about the decision with a heart yearning to obey and puts a message in God's monthly planner. The deadline, however, approaches with no clear leading, and a course has to be chosen according to frail judgment. Often my experience has been that faith was required of us at that beginning; clear leading would have precluded faith. Faith that God was aware of one's predicament and the approaching deadline, aware and able to guide us through the uncertainty. At that beginning there was no overawing sense of tranquility. Only in hindsight does one look back down the stairs and see the reason for that nagging inconvenience or that period of enforced waiting. He did guide, though when choosing the path the reins had felt slack.

Beginning to sense a call

A host of crazy, potent factors come into play as someone begins to sense a call to foreign missions. After years of dealing with people in the throes of all these emotions, mission boards can begin to sound cynical to applicants. The board views it as being firm, wise and realistic. They have seen it too often: a remote project in the hills has nine expatriot members. Eight of them look at their other colleague and see plainly that it would be better for him to go back into headquarters or another, easier posting. His health or his spirit or his personality clearly are not suited for this particular position. Common sense dictates it, prayer confirms it, and the group decides to confront the suffering brother with the reality of the situation. They care for his welfare. They love him, but the project is suffering also in his struggle to adjust. The work in the village, whatever that work may be, is hampered as increasing amounts of emotional reserves are expended by the others in the project to bandage the situation.

The confronted brother responds poorly. He feels attacked and abandoned. This goes deep into his sense of self respect, his most powerful will to achieve and persevere. The group's unanimous opinion forces him into a corner, and so he produces his trump card: the call of God.

The room grows hushed. By maintaining that God has called him to this particular place or posting, he is putting the rest of the team in an intolerable situation. Either they must say that their friend is wrong in this most sensitive area, or they are implying that God has made a ghastly mistake. The team is not ready to say either of these, and they plan instead new ways to support their brother. Everyone in the project tightens his or her belt another notch. The problem is not any closer to a solution. By definition, when an ailing missionary takes refuge in his perception of God's will against the judgment of other missionaries, help will always come too late, after needless violence has been done to everyone concerned.

Personnel selection at twelve thousand miles distance is a terrible, thankless task. To turn down an application appears to say, "Forget it. We do not believe that your experience of God's call is genuine." Rejections are worded more diplomatically; but if everyone insists on holding the view that God's call is a routinely certifiable piece of information, then there are but two alternatives. Everyone involved can agree pleasantly, or else there is going to be lots of painful disagreement over God's will. There is no middle ground.

An acquaintance of mine was executive director of a very prosperous mission. He once observed, "God certainly seems to call a lot of people to Nepal and very few to Bangladesh." Nepal is a small, exotic land with an intriguing culture; while Bangladesh is a crowded place, difficult and unsavory by any measure. Maybe there are other factors involved than God's true calling.

My experience of God's call into foreign missions was signally devoid of the whizbang, but I have learned to get over being embarrassed about it.

Very soon after my conversion I was struck by the obvious need for missionaries. It was as straightforward and unavoidable as a mathematical formula:

1. Jesus Christ is the Savior, not for any one particular culture, but for people of all cultures.

PLUS

2. Most of mankind has not had the opportunity to clearly hear the gospel about this Savior.

PLUS

3. Jesus commanded His disciples to preach about Himself to all cultures without exception.

EQUALS

I need to seriously consider being a missionary.

There was no need to wait for a supernatural call. A telex is nice, but not necessary.

I became a veterinarian because it seemed a good way for the likes of me to get involved in Third World agriculture. I was a product of the suburbs (the only time that I drove a tractor I managed to back it through a wall in the barn), but at the end of the years of study and practice I could glimpse opportunities in places closed to the typical church-planting, evangelistic missionary. It made for a dry, dusty beginning; not promising material for a made-for-TV movie.

"It just seemed the right thing to do, and so I did it."

I told this same story to the three men interviewing me to get into veterinary college—three white-coated strangers that held my future in the hands that were holding those clipboards. "Because I want to become a foreign missionary," seemed to be the least likely correct answer to the gruff, "And now son, why is it that you want to become a veterinarian?" It looked to be the best answer if my wish was to appear a flighty oddball and a poor investment. But I gave the answer anyway and in hindsight, found it to have been correct. There were two interview teams working through the applicants simultaneously. The group down in the library consisted of a bunch of tobacco-chewing good ol' boys who hated women and thought that God was the first half of what you shouted when you dropped a hammer on your bare foot. The group of interrogators that I was given upstairs in the pathology department was made up of two pious protestants and a devout Mormon. All three men had a place in their thinking to file my answer. If I had drawn the other interview team I would have been chewed up into very small pieces, mixed with tobacco juice and spit back out into the career search.

Evidence of God's guidance? I certainly count it as such, although I know that it leaves room for doubt if one wants to doubt. In any case, it was only obvious in hindsight.

I was called by God into missions at 11:47 Sunday morning, during the punch line of the sermon. I hit the office on Monday morning feeling joyful and full of purpose. There were angry clients to deal with, the computer crashed and I lost two-weeks' work. I still cannot get along with the business manager. By Thursday afternoon the world is back to normal; I am my usual self; and the sense of God's calling has faded into a bad joke. In a desperate attempt to retrieve that confident feeling I dial the 1-800 number of the denomination's mission board. The number is busy, however. Should I take this as an omen that God is not behind my attempt?

If one held this sort of view and did somehow manage to weather a selection process and gain the longed-for foreign shore, it would be poor preparation for life abroad. A six-round bout with amoebic dysentery, an unfriendly cultural experience while trying to wait in line at the foreign bank, a misconjugated verb with a hostile bureaucrat and reality would come clomping in without so much as wiping its dirty boots at the door.

Emotion burns hot, but it also burns quickly. It is poor fuel for the long haul.

We need a sense of God's call to see us through the times of black discouragement, but this sense must be deep, quiet, mature. It must survive the times of drought, when both call and purpose seem an unlikely mirage.

During college I was involved in the Christian Student Union. Some of us ran a "mission" outside of town in a poor little country church. We attracted about fifty little wiggly monsters every Friday evening. "Mission" consisted mostly of playing football with them until they were exhausted enough to go inside and listen to a Bible story. It was good practice for things later on.

One Friday we rented a school bus and took them into town for an evening of roller skating. I asked Joanne to come along as my date. And it was quite a first date. After two hours of "Shoot-the-Duck" and "the Hokey-Pokey," we packed them back into the bus and sent them home. Joanne and I went on for a quiet dinner.

I hesitate to share the following with single friends because they might expect their experience to be similar; but as we talked of ourselves that evening, Joanne mentioned that she was considering becoming a veterinarian in order to be able to work overseas. I am sure that she must have continued talking, but I could no longer hear her. As audible as a bell it seemed, came that impression that she was the one I was going to marry.

On a first date? Isn't that a bit melodramatic, a little unreliable? I can only say that I was sure. I did, however, have the foresighted wisdom not to mention my impression to Joanne for another four months.

It turned out later that she decided not to pursue being a veterinarian; she considered one in the family to be quite sufficient. Instead, she worked at the veterinary college and taught a generation of animal doctors how to put intravenous catheters into vicious, snappy Pekinese and Chihuahuas. She so endeared herself among the professors that I was known as Mr. Joanne St. Kilda.

We slogged through all of those years periodically forgetting and then recalling our overseas destination. After graduation we sighed, realizing that a year or two of practice before we went to serve was the wise thing to do. More preparation, more waiting. Most missionaries will confess, in their more sane moments, that it took much longer to arrive overseas than they had ever anticipated.

It was a slow route, but it was steady; there had been no major derailment . . . until Joanne, that dear, exceptional woman, contracted cancer.

We humbly heard, and yet did not hear, the surgeon as he tried to explain things to us from the other side, the healthy side, of his large beautiful desk. Then followed the sleep-walking months of surgery, radiation and chemotherapy.

God was kind, and she was healed; but I was left with a wife who should not leave the all-knowing care of Western medical technology. I was also left in a profession that I would have never chosen had I known that we were to live in the United States. The man so interested in serving Christ by serving Third World agriculture awoke to find his waiting room filled with poodles and pleasure horses.

"If this is how God treats His friends, no wonder He has so few."

I tried to not act like it (I got busy at church), but I was angry at God. Of course the world was in a mess if this was how His operation functioned. He needed people overseas, there were not enough to fill the vacancies, and yet He nailed me to an examination table in a prosperous part of town.

Where was God's will then? Where was the supposedly perfect purpose? As far as the eye could see, all was a dismal gray horizon, featureless in every direction. I could not have seen it then, but I was in training. Dismal, hopeless horizons are not such a bad place for prospective missionaries to invest some time; only no one chooses them voluntarily, and so they have to be thrust upon us.

After two long years filled with rabies shots and cats with kidney stones, I decided that if we were here to stay then we might as well set down roots. It was time to go sell my soul to some Mephistopheles working as a loan officer and buy a practice. We found the right one and things were progressing.

The final week of negotiations, our old friend at the Mission called. Just checking up after all these months and seeing if there was anything new in our situation. He had openings for veterinarians in Bolivia, Haiti and Dhurgastan.

I hung up the telephone and found that the world had slipped a few degrees on its axis during the short conversation. Negotiations for the practice continued to grind on from sheer momentum, but my heart was not in it.

And where was my heart? Why had this old scar opened again? Just when I had resigned myself to fate, old desires started moaning and rattling their chains. *Deus ex machina.* His timing is impeccable. The night before my new partner and I were to go lay down earnest money on the practice, I had to go over and explain that I could not go through with it. I felt like a scoundrel. Not only was I ruining my own career; I was shooting his with the same poisoned arrow.

The medical advice that we received took on a new character. It would be all right to go overseas—not outstanding but all right—as long as Joanne could receive frequent check-ups from a competent specialist. Suddenly we were back on track with a vengeance. The wasted years would prove their value later, and besides, I should count myself fortunate, many of God's servants spend decades offstage in the wilderness.

My call

"How did you experience God's call to be a missionary?"

Are people called to a particular organization, or is it by location? I'll go with anybody that can get me into Tibet. Is that how it works?

Well, it goes differently for different people. That is the

maddening thing about the entire process. There is no one space on the application form that fits the experience of every applicant. For some ardent souls it is Mimbwebwe or bust, for others it must be working with lepers and anywhere is fine with them. Joanne and I had certain qualities, and we had studied to obtain certain skills. All along our strategy was one of searching for the position that we could best fill. The continent or culture were not important to us. We chose a mission group that had experience in using veterinarians to good effect, but finding such an agency had not been easy.

We had attended the enormous Urbana Missions Conference in 1979, eager and expectant. I was confident that a vet was a very marketable commodity and that our major problem would be choosing from among the many clamoring offers.

They fed us through a computer that was supposed to link us with all of those missions that had opportunities for which we were suited. But our printout was very scanty.

Not giving in to discouragement, we next made our way over to the Armory where booth after booth of representatives were anxious to load people with publications about the work of their organizations.

"A veterinarian? What a good idea! No, we don't have any openings for a veterinarian, but there are bound to be lots of groups who do."

"No, not for a veterinarian right now. But you wouldn't happen to know something about agronomy would you? We have an opening for an agronomist in Mimbwebwe. . . ."

Our own denomination wanted to send us to Manila as part of a church-planting and discipleship team; not exactly what I had been preparing for in my seven years of college and two in clinical practice. Where was God's will? Where was the great need that everyone talked about?

Part of God's will is that His employees show some perseverance. We found the right organization, but it took some time. Then, it was their turn to show the perseverance. The director called me every couple of months and it was he who upset my plans to buy a practice.

"... places open in Bolivia, Haiti and Dhurgastan. Do you have a preference?"

Haiti: that would mean working with pigs, and I have precious little experience with them. Bolivia would be okay, I suppose. I knew a Bolivian once, and she was a wonderful person. Dhurgastan? All of my life I had wanted to see India or Nepal, and this sounded like both of them, only more so. I would like to live in Dhurgastan.

I held my breath, "No sir, no preference. You pray about it, and after seeing our paperwork, you decide for which we're best suited."

After two long days they called back to reveal our future. They considered us good candidates for Dhurgastan.

A clinical decision. There were emotions involved, plenty of them, but there were lots of other grimy factors involved and not solely a premonition of God's will. Does that make it any the less spiritual? To desire something more spiritual and other worldly is to want a God too unimaginative to become flesh Himself. Never belittle the supernatural, but do not make the opposite mistake either.

I'm a missionary

I could now, for better or for worse, tell people that I was a missionary when asked what was my "line."

Try this experiment some time: introduce yourself at a party as a veterinarian, and find out how many people have need of counsel about the health of their Yorkshire terrier.

Notice how popular and interesting and in demand you have become. Now, at the next party say that you are a Christian missionary and compare the reactions. At the second party you might as well admit that you are actively shedding the smallpox virus, a new one that is immune to the old vaccines. The reaction of the second party, whether it is a church potluck dinner or the sales staff from down at the firm, is not as different as one might expect.

It is a horrible thing, this sudden notoriety: to have been a normal guy and then to have been hurtled body and soul into higher religious realms.

Thursday, November 28, 1986

Had my first taste today of "full-timers" disease. Someone at the family's Thanksgiving party made a comment in front of me to Aunt Alice that had to deal with her anatomy. Off color, but no big deal. Alice, however, very nearly had a conniption. She covered my ears with her hands and reminded the other woman that "their little missionary" was present. The other woman then actually began to turn to me in apology. I replied that I had long noticed that portion of Alice but had never had the courage to comment.

But the damage was done; forever marked as fragile, stuffy and other-worldly. It made me want to cuss and spit just to prove myself one of the boys. The Pharisees, however, developed a taste for this sort of false respect; and so there must be danger lurking on either side of the sawhorse.

CHAPTER 2
_____

Not So Bon a Voyage

Leaving All Things Familiar

"Go and preach the Gospel; use words if necessary."
                                                St. Francis

Dear Friends,

I was definitely feeling odd: the goal of the whole exercise. Sickly sweet incense overpowered everyone in the room, and I was still recovering from a dinner of curried everything. The neat little Tibetan woman seated before me was pleasant, but her garbled English was hard to follow and added to my confusion. Around the room, the walls were painted bright ocher and green, the kind of colors I was told Buddhists enjoy. Napkin-sized prayer flags hung limply across the doors. My attention wandered to the picture on one side of the mantle, and I recognized the face and black-rimmed glasses of the Dalai Lama, spiritual leader of Tibet. To the other side of the mantle, in a similarly sized portrait was . . . but surely that was George Washington!

Joanne and I were visiting a Buddhist monastery in a restored house blocks away from the campus of the University of Washington. It was an evening designed to be cross-cultural, to put us in unfamiliar situations, part of our week-long orientation program at the Mission's headquarters in Seattle.

That week was a profitable time as we heard and saw everything from "an introduction to Hinduism" to what time our flight to Asia finally was to leave. Even more important was becoming acquainted with the staff at headquarters, the people who would labor to keep us working in the field. There is a lot of work necessary to support projects in the Third World. We were impressed and relieved; it was nice to see the commitment of this supporting staff, to put faces to what had only been voices on a telephone.

Joanne and I are now thick in the process of deputation, raising prayer and financial support for our three-year term as veterinary missionaries to the nation of Dhurgastan. Also, we are busy packing and facing the awful task of deciding what to take, what to sell, what to simply give away. All of those sweatshirts bought on vacation through the years, Joanne's collection of onyx donkeys . . .

We were late in boarding our plane for the return flight from Seattle, so late that the standbys were going down the ramp to the jet. We were given the last two seats aboard, our consolation being that we were "bumped-up" into first class.

Our seats were on the same airplane and were going to the same destination, but it was definitely different from conditions back in the tourist portion of the cabin. First class was secluded, far from the screaming turbines. There was ample leg room and the stewardesses doted over us as if we were celebrities; perhaps they were unaware that we were counterfeits and had done nothing to deserve the special attention. We were paupers playing at millionaires.

The best part of the scam was the food. We chose filet mignon from the menu, and it came in garnished courses rather than as one cellophane-wrapped nutritional unit thrown at us from the aisle by a busy crewmember.

By the time dessert appeared, I was accustomed to luxury and expected it as my constitutionally guaranteed right. As Joanne and I were poised for an eager assault on our hot fudge sundaes, a fellow from the back of the plane lurched past us. His eyes widened in comic disbelief at our feast. He was about my equal in age and had definitely bought the same tourist ticket that we had; but he had to sway back down the aircraft, never again to be satisfied with his lot aboard the plane.

Now I agree with J.R.R. Tolkien and normally dislike allegory. Some author considers himself cute and subtle, as he steps down from his soapbox, picks it up and beats his readers about the head and shoulders with it. Nevertheless, in the experience aboard that flight I was faced with a dreadful picture of my entire life.

Here in the United States I have always been in first class compared to the lion's share of humanity which lives in the undeveloped nations. I am aboard the same airplane as they, have the same creature needs and ultimately must choose from between the same destinations. I expect affluence as my due and can barely make myself remember that I have done nothing virtuous to deserve my physical and spiritual plenty. I would never admit to anything so crass, but somewhere inside I consider myself superior to all of the "peasants" on board. If they were hard up, then somewhere along the line they must have left something important undone. A kind of Christian doctrine of Karma; the mistake in thinking which Job's friends made.

Friends, we have done nothing to warrant God's blessings. We may be more educated than others, but that does not necessarily mean smarter. We may be more wealthy, but we do not work any harder. We are saved from ourselves and from God's anger by the gift of His Son. We are not, however, more righteous in our own pathetic efforts.

Your partner,
Martin

The long process

The pages of my pocket calendar turned relentlessly, as if a fan was blowing them. The great adventure of living overseas approached. As it got nearer, one could see blemishes on its complexion that had not been noticeable from further away. Those blemishes brought new fears, which in their turn brought insomnia and hot, nighttime tears. My journal of the time is filled with the image of roots being torn out from clinging soil. Not one of the atlases and tourist pamphlets and *National Geographic* articles could make Dhurgastan feel like a homecoming. Joanne and I had briefly met one couple that lived there and worked in the Mission. Two acquaintances and eleven million strangers, hardly encouraging odds.

People are usually surprised by how difficult it is to get overseas in a missionary position. After finding the right organization and leaping through the fiery hoops of an interview process, next came the hurdles of preparing to go. Had God's call turned into muscle yet?

There are jobs to quit and possessions to sell, more possessions than you had realized even though you knew that you had more possessions than you had realized. You had never seen yourself in the role of a grasping, greedy materialist until it came to disposing of it all. Your wardrobe, the station wagon, that motorcycle that you should've never bought. The couch you won at the furniture store, the desks and lamps; do you keep what is inside the filing cabinet? And what is to be done with the globe I gave Joanne for Christmas last year?

One is suddenly something of a minor celebrity, somewhere between the local television weatherman and a first term congressman; but do not bother getting used to the notoriety. It brightens and fades like a streaking meteorite. There are endless farewell dinners to eat; people who missed your presentation on Wednesday night want to arrange a private viewing in their home. There are more Sunday school classes that want to hear you speak than there are remaining Sundays.

November 30
I must use my time extremely well this next week. We move from Austin to my parents' house in just two weeks. We go to Dhurgastan in thirty-six short days. What an astonishing thought, yet at the same time it is nonsensical to me. There is apparently no nerve for the sensation which that thought is meant to trigger. It is like a referred pain. During a heart attack a man feels shooting pains coursing up and down his left arm. He has never been much aware of his heart before and so his brain interprets the incoming pain to be from the arm, instead of the ischemic heart muscle. Going to Dhurgastan in the same way leaves me numb. I've read the statistics, seen the pictures . . . but nothing. I cannot process it. What is it like to be away from friends, family and all things familiar for three years? I

suppose all this means that my culture shock will be devastating.

December 14

I am very distressed today. Everyone around me seems
self-absorbed in their little, trivial interests. I honestly do
not believe that the swarm of wild emotions careening
around inside of me is a result of hurt feelings over less
attention and sympathy than I think that I deserve. It's just
that our strange situation brings with it a different viewpoint, much like Joanne's diagnosis of cancer did. What
Charles Williams brilliantly called "the illusion of mor-
tality" gets ripped away. No one bothers to see from
another's viewpoint, another perspective from which different things loom large in the changed foreground.
Everyone, instead, is concerned with their own problems,
major and minor. I'm afraid that I'll reach Dhurgastan
already spent emotionally and physically—these last two
weeks of wining and dining and leave-taking have been
brutal.

January 6

Despite all of our efforts to be organized, there was last
minute packing to be done. God again proved His last
minute timing as well. We sold our car "Tigger" to a couple
of Christian fellows on the very last day. Had dinner at
Pino's with my folks and Joanne's mother. Conversation
revolved around trying to figure out the international date
line; also ate lots of pasta, the carbohydrate loading phase
of our anti-jet lag diet. Moved all of the trunks over to my
folks' in the Mercedes; listened to the lite-rock station as I
drove. At every song I thought, "This is the last time I'll be
hearing this." To bed well after one o'clock. First sound to

reach me the next morning at five a.m. was muffled thunder. For some reason it had never occurred to me that it could rain on the day that we were to leave.

Saying goodbye

It is needless to write about how much I detest goodbyes. Everyone detests them. These however, had to be endured. There was Joanne's mother, sad and not able to fully grasp the purposes behind Christian missions. She was making a brave attempt to not resent me for taking her daughter to the other side of the planet. Aunt Aspa had spoken honestly for the rest of the family, "Okay, you two, go on and do what you want for the next three years, because after that you must come back and do what we want you to." Dear old Aspa; she was to die before we returned for our first furlough.

My father was familiar with missions and missionaries. His father had been a Baptist preacher in rural Northern Texas and he had been filling out the little blue and white Lottie Moon Christmas offering envelopes all of his life. He understood the need for missions, but this did not translate somehow into our own situation. He had called me one evening in Austin. He knew that the job had to be done; what he was not so sure of was just exactly why it had to be us to do it.

Why must you go? (We heard this often.) There are enough poor people here that need help. Why not stay and spread the gospel among them?

The loudspeaker crackles and a calm woman in a red blazer speaks into a microphone at the check-in desk. "Please have your boarding passes ready." How can she be so casual when we are leaving everything and everyone that we have ever known?

Walking down the ramp Joanne begins to cry; as she turns around for a last, lingering glimpse of our friends, I take her firmly by the arm. "Don't" was the single word of command I said fiercely and then led the way into the airplane.

It is still hard for me to know all of what was involved in that moment on the entrance ramp, but it was symbolic of much to come. Joanne needed sympathy as she strove to cope with the flood of changes. I coped by being tough and refusing to give her any tenderness. My iron-man exterior covered a heart even more frightened than hers. Were I to open the door one crack to all of my hurting, I was afraid that there would be no closing it again. "Don't" was how I would respond to many things over the next three years.

No chance to adjust

Ask missionaries and they will tell you how much they hate airplanes. Those infernal machines are horrible for one's psychological well-being.

Earlier generations of missionaries survived much greater rigors than their modern heirs. If there was a furlough in store for them, it could easily be a decade away. The Jesuit fathers in Rajdhani have only recently begun a policy containing a home leave; prior to that, they expected to live their lives in Dhurgastan without ever returning. Earlier missionaries were built of firm stuff. They did, however, have the luxury of an ocean voyage.

Oh, those voyages could be dangerous, no doubt—storms off of the dark coast, typhoons in the Pacific; but they brought as well some blessed advantages. Those of us who board airplanes are still licking our wounds from gory goodbyes, when a ridiculously short twenty-four hours later we deplane to face a new world of clamoring hellos. No chance of adjustment; the two in-flight movies were more annoying than comforting.

A tedious ocean voyage offered time with which to bundle up the memories of home. Once this painful chore was finished, there remained plenty of time in which to consider the approaching future.

I have been both seasick and jet-lagged in my life, and prefer the slow, thoughtful turn around the Cape of Africa.

CHAPTER 3

Orienting to the Orient

First Impressions

"Very nearly, but not quite exactly opposite of what I expected."

Anonymous

It turned out that there was no need to forsake all of Western culture at the door of our Thai Airlines' flight. A group of very friendly, black American men were in the row of seats in front of us. Somewhere between Seattle and Tokyo they introduced themselves to me as the Coasters, authors of such immortal music as "Charlie Brown" and "Yackity-Yack."

Dear Friends,

People want different things from a monthly prayer letter. Some require it to be "newsy," hoping to hear of our quaint adventures and daily circumstances. Others desire something more "metaphysical," great insights into reality now that Joanne and I have crossed the seas. I hope our letters will be something of both. Mostly, I hope that they assist you in lifting our ministry up before God.

News Department: Goodbyes to family and friends were

hard; but other than that, our trip to Dhurgastan was safe and uneventful. We spent one night in humid, throbbing Bangkok and ate breakfast with our Asian area director; then we made the flight to Rajdhani, capital of Dhurgastan!

Customs was bothersome but not the persecution that some have encountered; and our "link family" with the Mission met us just outside and helped us to bicker with luggage porters.

Two days later our family took us on the mailbus for the two hundred-kilometer ride to Bhadrapur, which, after language school, is the village where we shall be living. We traveled on the "highway" which I suspect received its name from the anxious missionary's, "This is way too *high*, and there ain't no *way*." Crawling along the hilly road with its patchy cement, too narrow for traffic to drive abreast, the short distance took us nine hours.

In Bhadrapur, Mel and Fiona Lewis took over caring for the fledgling arrivals. Mel, you may remember, is the veterinarian whose place I shall be taking, and I was glad of the chance to see a course like the one I shall be teaching next autumn. I listened for two weeks as he and Elizabeth (a British vet) taught fifteen Dhurgastani farmers everything from rudimentary parasitology to obstetrics. At least I assumed from their actions and teaching aids that those were the topics; the whole experience was a tremendous incentive for my language studies. And after my abysmal record in high school Latin, I needed plenty of incentive.

We are now back in Rajdhani waiting to move in with a Dhurgastani family and begin language classes in earnest in early February. Already we have met wonderful missionary colleagues from Holland, Germany, Australia, lots from the United Kingdom, Canada, Ghana and South Africa.

Metaphysical Department: Dhurgastan on first impression has been very much like and completely different from what I expected. Though Nepal has Mount Everest, Dhurgastan has seven of the world's ten tallest peaks. This is what it is famous for, and because of it, I expected something like a primitive Switzerland, poor but quaint and alpine. Orientation sessions in Seattle dealt so extensively with culture shock that I am mortified to have fallen victim to it. Everything external has been changed; for this I was reasonably prepared. It was internal changes that caught me like a blitzing linebacker. "All the props have been knocked out" is a phrase I've heard, and have used myself, several times our first month here. I begin to guess at how very much God must first accomplish in me before there is any question of His accomplishing something through me. At home, surrounded by loving friends and their high expectations, it is easy to pantomime Christian maturity. Here imitations simply melt in the heat.

One early morning I was overcome by the sense of the unfamiliar and the uncomfortable. I was riding through the cold, predawn fog in the back of a rickety auto-rickshaw, planning how I would escape. I could leave Joanne a note, take the remainder of the traveler's checks and go standby on the next glistening white airliner out at the airport. . . .

Full of self-pity, I noticed my shivering cabbie in front of me. What prospects had he? This life was no chosen adventure on his part. He could not opt out and retreat to a safe homeland. No one was going to send him off at the first signs of serious stress. Why, even his rick-shaw was on it last legs, coughing asthmatically up a gentle hill.

I wore my thick down parka—he had only a tattered sweater and scarf. Worst of all, he has not the hope of Jesus Christ in his heart.

I listened to the gagging engine. We'll stay awhile longer yet.

Your partner,
Martin St. Kilda

There were many things at which that prayer letter did not hint. One's supporters, for their part, do not actually want the entire messy truth; and you, for your part, are not strong enough to give it to them anyway. People like to support winners and people like to pretend that they are winners.

It did not, for one thing, hint at how sick I was when I wrote it. We had not been in Asia three days before some nasty microbe that I had not met came up and introduced himself to my immune system in no uncertain terms. I shivered with fever in the classroom in Bhadrapur, watching the chalkdust swirl through a sunbeam. I listened to everyone speak Basha and tried to laugh when they did; a silly farce of an exercise, of course. Everyone knew that I was a mute newcomer. The morning I began to feel better, I got food poisoning, a disease notoriously difficult to pretend is not there for the benefit of one's host.

The letter also contained no reference to the surprises of our first night in Rajdhani.

January 6
Awoke to a great commotion of loud voices and slamming

doors, a sensation made all the worse in that the voices spoke an unknown language. I had absolutely no idea of the time because my mind was still en route and was hanging somewhere over the mid-Pacific. It would be several days before the claim check was found and it was reunited with my body. (Our anti-jet lag diet had proven to be some hopeful figment of the State Department's fertile imagination.)

Our hosts banged on the door like Gestapo agents do in old war movies and shouted that a next door neighbor had died. Would we watch their daughters until they got back?

Well, of course we would. The oldest of the little girls was four. She was very shy with strangers, but chances were that she would sleep through the whole incident.

She slept through all of the commotion of arriving neighbors and hollered advice. She woke up when her parents shut the door in their departure. There was no way to console her, confronted as she was in the middle of the night by two strangers. Amy turned her face into a corner and screamed non-stop for what seemed like two days but could not have been a minute over two hours.

Our hosts returned, and after quieting Amy were able to give us good news. A little girl, a cousin of the Dhurgastani family over the wall, was visiting from her home in the remote hills. She had left some coals burning in her bedroom to stave off the capital's cold night air. This is a common practice in the villages, but the cement houses of these city-slickers are much more airtight than the mud and thatch of the hill people. The coals had consumed the oxygen in the room where she was sleeping. It had been a close call. The family heard her claw once at the door before she had fainted. Some time on an oxygen mask at the nearby mission hospital had been enough for a speedy recovery.

The problem of traffic

Traffic in Asia never fails to leave a lasting impression. My mother had once befriended a woman from India at the international ladies group at our church. As loyal patriots we had wanted to know what thing she was most enamored with about America. We expected a compliment about our representative form of government. Or perhaps, if not the philosophical sort, she would choose our insanely successful brand of capitalism; but her reply left us disappointed and confused. She said that she liked our traffic and made the cryptic remark that here people obeyed traffic lights and stayed in their lanes.

She must be pulling our legs. Was this some clever affront? Of course we obey traffic lights; what is the alternative? I've seen my Dad stop at a red light for three minutes on an absolutely deserted road at four in the morning when we were going duck hunting.

I now confronted the alternative. The woman's words came back to me like last month's credit card bill, though they must have been spoken fifteen years earlier.

Dhurgastani traffic is beyond words—a horrible thing for a book, but I must push on and try to describe it anyway. It must be survived to be believed, but the risk probably is not worth it. That nation's borders were closed to the outside world for a century and a half by a string of tyrannical prime ministers. These draconian policies kept Queen Victoria's Raj at bay, but they also successfully kept out every shred of progress. In Bhadrapur, the ox cart, well known to Ramses the Great in Egypt, was new technology as recently as 1930. Dhurgastan is, therefore, a nation of confirmed pedestrians which has suddenly inherited the diesel truck, bypassing all of the many stages in between.

Traffic is a constant din of competing horns, and for good reason. The recognized principle is that one cannot possibly be considered responsible for an accident if one managed to honk the horn before impact. Our second day, while riding behind my host on a motorcycle, I had considered him very rude listening to his constant bleep-bleeping, that is until he explained the principle. He told me, quite seriously, that if forced to choose, he would rather his brakes fail than his horn.

The vehicles among which one competes to be heard are a complete assortment, no two similar. The streets of Rajdhani act as a sort of elephant graveyard for ancient Toyotas. When the things become unlicensable in Haiti and Costa Rica, they immigrate to Dhurgastan and do another hundred thousand miles' service as taxi-cabs.

Holy cows, wearing the heavy-lidded expression appropriate to Hindu sadhus, wander the streets oblivious to the melee. Bicycles, with three adults aboard, streak by, the riders looking like escapees from a circus act with the ringmaster hot in pursuit. Assorted tractors belch by, buses donated by the Japanese, electric trams that shower sparks down onto the crowds waiting to clamber into them, the wonderful Tata trucks from India all painted up in devotion to some god or goddess.

All do their part to keep up a braying, ringing, smoking melee that paralyzes the newcomer. No point looking one direction for oncoming traffic; it could be coming from any sector at any moment. Traffic policemen in their immaculate white gloves and leggings (also Japanese donations) are too wise to get involved, and lounge on the sidewalks. I suppose were a pedestrian to be run over, they might leap into decisive action, but this is speculation, and I do not know it to be true.

It was only much later that I had to concede, without taking back one word of the above, that the system of no-system appeared to work remarkably well and that one was much more likely to be involved in a serious accident in Columbus, Ohio, or Eugene, Oregon. It is up to the urban planners to glean whatever lesson that contains.

The problem of communication

Those first, speechless days in Rajdhani, Joanne and I felt tethered to our hosts by a very short umbilicus. The thought of even a short stroll out in that traffic, in a city without street signs and among people with whom I could not communicate was terrifying. So much for my prized ability to handle cross-cultural situations. Those had all been Portuguese or Chinese students over for Thanksgiving dinner. That was on my turf! The way I reasoned, were I to turn a corner and lose my host's house from direct visual contact, then I might as well lay down before one of the speeding trucks bringing firewood into the city. That way at least the end would be quick. No hassle for the truck driver; he'd bleep his horn and not be responsible. I'd never know, but others would find out if the policemen would jump into decisive action.

"The days creep by on all fours like weeks," I wrote to my parents that first Saturday. When one is in a new environment where one does not know the rules by which anything is done acceptably, then one must apply conscious consideration to even the smallest act. Nothing can be done off-handedly and out of routine. Simple tasks can become major tests.

I had never been confronted by an Asian toilet before. This was no fault of mine, having never been to Asia; it had never occurred to me to ask anyone, having no reason to expect a new kind of toilet. By definition, one never knows the questions to ask; and this rule held fast in my case. By the time I realized that I was in need of some explanations, I was in no position to go and ask for one. And it is the sort of thing which seasoned missionaries forget that has the potential of being intimidating. The scene is set for a catastrophe that will recur over and over again, an initiation for every greenhorn.

Conscious attention given to every detail, learning all day long, has the unanticipated effect of slowing the passage of time. This is why fifteen minutes seems an eternity to toddlers. Asking a two–year–old to wait until after the television show is over is as if someone asked the father to call back—this time next year.

The problem of housing

Our career in Dhurgastan very nearly lasted only one day. We dropped Joanne and the six trunks off at the house of our link family. Then I was driven across town to the Mission's headquarters to telex North America of our safe arrival and to open a bank account. Headquarters came as a sad surprise: palm yellow, second-rate buildings, and so squalid. At sight of my new organization, I began to repent of all of the years wasted trying to get myself overseas.

I was introduced to a few people in a dizzying way; no plan, just whoever we happened to bump into in the courtyard or the business office. I signed all of the pink forms laid before me in triplicate; then back into the weary Volkswagen van with the side door that the passenger had to hold closed during a left turn.

This was a strategic mistake. Up until this point I had only witnessed prosperous squalor. Driving through the narrow back streets, we crossed the river down near the ghats where the dead Hindus are cremated, past the garbage dump where dogs and crows and human scavengers with burlap sacks scrambled over the rancid mountain of decay. This was real squalor, world-class filth. My nose registered a disgust that was off the olfactory gauges.

The really disturbing thing was that we were headed for the house in which we were to live for the five months of language school. The awful sights which flashed by on this first afternoon could be meditated on at length as we pedaled through the area on our Hero brand bicycles.

We had wanted to live with a Dhurgastani family in order to learn as much as we could in the brief five months. Our room was at the top of the ladder, on the third floor. It was about the size of a largish American bathroom with a dirt floor and a ceiling so low that I could not stand up to my full height in any part of the room. Two wires were wound about hooks and then disappeared up the wall and into the tin roof. These wires, it was translated for me, were a great improvement added recently. The last time that a missionary had lived in the room, the entire roof had blown off in one of those fierce spring storms that roll off of the shoulders of the Himalayas and rampage through Rajdhani. Her belongings had been blown all over the surrounding potato fields.

Three weeks later, we moved into the little room and considered ourselves fortunate and well looked after. By that time we had adjusted our idea as to what constituted unacceptable levels of squalor, and the place appeared homey and quite liveable. But fresh from the hearth of American wealth, on that first day when it seemed so clear that I had managed to ruin the rest of my life, the room looked like something designed by the Turkish prison system. It made me want to go home after about three hours on Dhurgastani soil. If I had to wait a day or two for the flight, I would do so at the Hilton. If Joanne stuck it out and would not come home with me, we would keep up a lively correspondence and I would wish her all the best.

And where was God in all of this?

I was not grumbling over the problem of evil or shaking an angry fist at bronze heavens. I was not bothered by one part of the earth living in bloated affluence while the other picked its livelihood out of garbage. Those are questions for idealists, and I had suddenly given up all of my ideals. No, I was no longer concerned for others; this was every man for himself. How could God have allowed me—good old educated, upper middle class me—to have made this drastic mistake? More importantly, how was He going to get me out of this? Three years in these conditions were completely out of the question!

The problem of tourism

Dhurgastan, these well-traveled days, is on the tourist trail. Those who like to wear wrinkled khaki clothes and "rough it" for a good time, come and trek between tourist lodges along well-marked paths. When they grow tired of roughing it, they return to their normal lives with a carousel of slides to show friends.

Joanne and I like khaki clothes, but we often pondered why it was that tourists rave over the beauties of Dhurgastan; they see the alpine wonderland, while we always found it deadly depressing. The nearest thing to an answer that we have found was the lesson of that first bleak afternoon.

Had I been on vacation those new sights, even the horrific ones, would have been fascinating and best seen through a viewfinder. More trophies for the slide projector. But coming there to live and work seemed to change the lenses through which we perceived things. This was my new home. Poverty makes a great story, but not so great a next door neighbor.

Trekkers often found me a wet blanket-clad killjoy. "Why are you here then if you cannot stand the place?"

Well, for a different reason. We did not come because we liked it, not even for the adventure of enduring hardship. I frequently reminded myself that were the place idyllic and the people progressive and uniformly delightful, there would be that much less reason for us to be there. All the sights and sounds were disquieting; I had known that it had to be so. Where God's Spirit is foreign, there even wealth is rotten; how much more so poverty?

I had not known things were going to be this bad, but that could not be called "shock." That surprise was only a matter of degree; things that I knew were to be bad were merely worse than I had expected.

The problem of first impressions

The "shock," the real crushing punch to the solar plexus that left me writhing for breath, was the first impression of my missionary colleagues. Those that did not look odd were downright ugly. Their clothes were not right and their mannerisms were distressing. I had given up everything dear and familiar, had cast myself onto their bosom for solace and fellowship, and they all acted cool and preoccupied. Didn't they know how to make someone feel welcome? Weren't they aware of the fears with which I was wrestling?

At Bhadrapur I introduced myself to a missionary who was taking the animal health course along with the Dhurgastani farmers. Talk turned to her post at the boarding school in that village. "Ach, I hate it. Can't stand the children." A thin Scottish woman with short white hair and a weather-beaten face, she said the words in a particularly convincing manner. Over the course of the years, Stoney was to become a very dear friend; and I was privileged to gain access behind the scenes of that crusty exterior, but that first meeting left me despondent. She was about as full of the joy of the Lord as a frozen fish.

This missionary foible of the bad first impression became intelligible to me slowly, as I obtained it myself. There are several reasons behind it. First, missionaries are people like anyone else, and are not all by nature sunny extroverts. The sad lesson of church life anywhere is that after the first Sunday, it is the visitor who must reach out and find his niche in the congregation. Likewise, missionaries are busy people laboring beneath many expectations; and they assume that someone else will take the responsibility of comforting the new arrivals and explaining to them about Asian toilets.

There is something of the fraternity house atmosphere among missionaries as well. They do not mean to be cruel about it, but there it is. Everyone is instinctively aware of who in the room has seniority, who has been in the country the longest, has the most difficult assignments, has the best use of the language. "Oh yes, he is just beginning his third term. You know, don't you, that she was in India for nine years prior to coming to Dhurgastan. . . ." Everyone is expected to carve his own initials, to prove her own mettle.

No time to baby the precious little dears; goodness knows, no one ever did me. After all, the best way to learn to swim is to be thrown off of the pier and into the surf.

But the most important reason that missionaries can seem unsociable after the initial handshake is rarely mentioned, even among themselves. It is too painful, too near the core.

They live an uprooted life. They have all cried in airports, maybe numerous times. They have been cast out into remote locations with only a handful of others like themselves, and they had no hand in choosing these new friends. In our Mission, one's colleagues were more than likely from a different country and church background. Even those supposedly most like you were very different. Your new friends eat hot custard after every meal (and think it a splendid treat), call jello "jelly" and confuse football and soccer.

In spite of the vast differences, however, they do draw near, by God's grace, in that special fellowship that is experienced by mountain climbers, infantrymen and foreign missionaries. Shared dangers, the common adversary, communal success and failure. And by some unseen law, just when those relationships become soft and warm like a good plaid shirt, someone gets transferred. Or someone gets a bad case of hepatitis and needs to recover at home, or a baby is born with hydrocephalus and requires urgent care back in England. Please pack our things for us in two groups: one is to be the good things that we would want sent back to us if we find that we are not coming back; the other, things we would not want back in Europe and you can sell for us in the village. Give all the money to the Bible society. God bless you . . .

The rupture of all of your close friendships is only a telegram away. People leave on furlough intending to return but do not. Then some starched newcomer arrives in the village needing help and is filled with silly questions, a replacement for reliable old so-and-so who everyone knows was irreplaceable. And would people expect you to hold the hands of the newcomer? Well, forget it. I'm not going to reach out and get burned again. I'll be civil but not intimate.

If they should want to get to know me, they know my address.

With time, however, starch gets worn off and again begins that wonderful brotherhood of the common life; only you cannot explain the whole of this process to someone fresh off of the Thursday flight from Bangkok.

February 22

Dear Folks,

Thank you for your frequent letters, frequent prayers and sacrificial level of support that keep us encouraged and able to live in Dhurgastan. Things will settle down soon enough and the law of "out-of-sight-out-of-mind" will begin to take its toll. The one, lone, good point about this is that correspondence will then require less of my time.

One of the few things that I genuinely miss is that neither of you two are here to share a morning's experiences with us, to see the wonders and the sufferings, so that we could speak of them; but also in order that we could just feel them without any need to talk. Mom needs to visit our out-of-doors toilet which Joanne has termed "the pit of death." Dad needs to talk with Anglicans of the "high-church" persuasion and read the *Bhagavad Gita* with me, to decide how best to respond to the begging lepers, to consider the experiences of Gandhi (I highly recommend the book about him by E. Stanley Jones—a Christian evangelist who knew him). To discover together how to get involved with our Dhurgastani congregation that has seen so many white faces come and go, to struggle with poor language aptitude and the fear of going out and conversing with people in the street who speak too rapidly . . .

It goes on and on: to feel the New Testament's parables rise off of the page for a "first generation church"; to bicycle around Rajdhani on its Ring Road and see the not-so-distant Himalayas burn vivid orange behind the lower dusky purple hills; to eat the smog of an Indian night bus with as many people bundled on the roof as inside; to weave crazily through a herd of plodding cows in a runaway three-wheeled motorcycle. I hope that you don't object to this stream-of-consciousness letter. I find the technique very liberating. Snapshots of our new life, resisting the details in favor of the perceptions.

To experience Third World bureaucracy when trying to pick up a load of books in back of the airport; to turn a corner and find the Democracy Day parade upon you in rank upon rank of soldiers, politicians and school children; frumpy-looking cymbal crashing bands—and scores of other people that you could not decide why, or if they were included in the procession.

To receive letters from loved ones on the other side of the world—they write of things which now seem remote enough to have occurred in one's "previous existence"; to eat downstairs in the crumbly old kitchen with our Dhurgastani family; to have old wrinkled women glare at you no matter how you do anything; to taste things that resemble nothing that has ever accosted your taste buds before. We need to awaken together and pray in the dark by the light of a single candle and listen to the noise of predawn Asia outside—men and women hacking with tuberculosis, old diesels being beaten into life. Or lie in bed as night pulsates outside in the barking of ten thousand distant dogs, and sitar music undulates over cheap speakers at the corner shop. Your warm wife, already asleep, cuddles next to you under the blanket as you consider your future prospects and your past mistakes, and you wonder how you came to be here with the rats doing aerobic workouts above you and causing the dirt to fall between the bamboo matting. You must try to make friends with the dirty little children who wiggle their way unafraid into your lap, to be the first person to ever give the family dog a friendly pat instead of a vicious kick, to watch the baby goats frolic in the courtyard next door before they are chased inside the neighbor's house to spend the night safe from the jackals that come up from the river.

Please come and listen to wise old missionary women speak with experience about spiritual warfare; come sense Christ's love for yourself and for poor Asia; come be overcome by the needs around you and learn how your childhood in the USA had nothing about it of reality. Close your eyes and pray to leave by the next clean, white Thai airliner so that you can get "normal" again. Throw your whole life on the altar for Christ and vow to never return to the West. Be thankful for the prayers and support of others who sent you. Feel miserable for being the same old reprobate that you were at home, entirely unfit and unreliable. Listen to the BBC together at the Mission's guesthouse and after hearing about the stupid waste in the Middle East, never care to hear the news again. Get excited that "Stars and Stripes" beat the Aussies four to zip in the America's Cup only to realize with a gasp that the budget for one of those silly yachts could finance all of the hospitals in Dhurgastan for two years. Meet Christians who disagree with you on theology, yet hold their position with such compassion and sincerity that you begin to fear that there is no way to know the truth, even His truth.

Come and fear that all of your precious professional knowledge is not enough. Turn around and want to treat all of the tormented animals that you see every day. Watch an ugly sow savage one of her own piglets as two puppies romp playfully over their patient mother.

Rambo and Madonna posters steam and flex from tearoom walls, old pilgrims in dusty saffron robes carry the trident of Shiva and beg from door to door, fruit sellers hawk their wares, and grandmothers are bent double under a load of firewood on their backs that would cripple a Marine. Women bathing in the river, nursing filthy babies, working hard, are frightened enough by your white face to throw a shawl over their heads and run away.

Get splashed by the immaculate car of a speeding diplomat; give half a penny to a begging old hag after having just spent five dollars on an unneeded book. Encounter Dhurgastanis educated in America who harbor a completely unthought-of perspective on your country, and on all of history, for that matter.

Feel physically fit; feel like you are going to die and wish that the process would hurry up. Watch as a fellow tries to steal your wife's bicycle while her back is turned; have another man on a crowded bus, against all local custom, rise and give her his seat. Glory in the little bird that chatters on the windowsill, the one that doesn't have any glass in it. Watch a mongoose out hunting in the potato fields. Laugh when you learn that the owl, considered the wisest of birds in your culture, is thought of as retarded here because it sleeps all day.

Arrive at language school, all soggy tweed, on a rainy morning. Wouldn't you like to give away all of your possessions and live like a native? Wouldn't it be great to be back in Austin in that plush theater, sipping on an icy Coke and watching "Out of Africa" again? Those were the days when cultural experiences were all romance and no sweat.

Good and bad, cozy and uncomfortable, straightforward and confounding. Pleasant, unimaginable, worthwhile, appealing and revolting. Awesome, petty and everything in between and besides.

I doubt that I shall ever be quite the same again, and that is not altogether a happy thought for me. By God's grace I shall be an improved me, but I begin to see how and why missionaries always appear to be so out of step. But then, how can a returning war veteran describe a steamy jungle's fire-fight to his old high school sweetheart?

Your son,
Martin

CHAPTER 4

Justifiable Homicide

Language Acquisition

"Oh, don't be such an idiom!"

Wade Bradshaw

Dear Friends,

Joanne and I are now in the middle of the promised "honeymoon" period with our new, adopted culture. There are still plenty of tense, uncertain moments; but, for the most part, we are enjoying the exotic surroundings. Many of you have written to assure us of your prayers on our behalf, and, very sincerely, I can say that we sense God's gracious answers daily.

Language Department: We are up to our vocal chords in intensive study of Basha, the major language of Dhurgastan. We've conquered the alphabet in ten days; so that now, as I bicycle through Rajdhani, signs that once looked like birds' tracks on a muddy riverbank are coming into focus—some of them appear to even say something. Pronunciation is, however, an entirely different matter. As I wrote to our church in Austin, speaking Basha is a wee bit like playing the harmonica with your feet. (You might try to do this sometime in a crowded music store to have a simulated cross-cultural experience.)

Our language class is a small group of twenty, made intimate by common goals, stresses and commitment. We have drawn very close to one another like newborn piglets do in a cold barn.

Housing Department: We have moved in with a precious Dhurgastani family of four and occupy a room on the top floor of their house. At the southwest corner of Rajdhani, we can look out of our window and watch families hoe their fields until the sun sets behind the hazy hills.

Little six-year-old Priya is our best language tutor by far. She, like most six-year-olds, never tires of repetition. Instead of boredom, repetition produces in her a sense of accomplishment. Whereas an adult loses patience after saying something twice, not so our Priya. She will continue on and on merrily until I begin to near comprehension. She is also ideal in that she knows no English. Being tutored by a six-year-old, of course, is not without its pitfalls.

Adventure Department: One night as usual Priya trooped upstairs to our room to see what the giant strangers were doing. I was scribbling a letter. She pointed to my glasses on the table and clearly enunciated "kasko."

I put the letter aside. We language students must learn to take advantage of opportunities on their own schedule. I asked her to repeat. "Kasko," came the unmistakable reply. I jotted this dutifully into the little notebook I keep for my expanding vocabulary, pleased with the acquisition. An enthusiastic language learner must use new words frequently to make them "his own." We must actively seek out chances to utilize our knowledge, however great or small. One cannot wait for fluency to arrive before going out and initiating conversations. We make our feeble attempts as we go through stores, wait with women around the tap outside or are smashed in a crowded bus.

When someone understands and responds to some memorized portion of gobbledygook, it is a marvelous, magical feeling, as if huge gates creaked open upon our nervous command of "abracadabra." But "kasko" was never one of my winners. People shook their heads and gave me the look which I normally reserve for the two-headed goats I occasionally deliver. I would point at bifocals perched atop the bridge of some dignified person's nose and say it, but it never went any further.

Only later, so much later that I shudder to think about it, did Priya's father correct me. Priya had not been saying "glasses" but rather something to the effect of "Hey, whose are those anyway?"

Would anyone like to buy a slightly used harmonica?

Your partner,

Martin

Verbal communication

The experience of foreign missionaries is a relationship between ratios and goes something like this: enjoyment of one's new homeland and the sense of doing something useful there are directly proportional to how well one can verbally communicate with the people. The same ratio described differently reads: one's happiness is inversely proportional to the difficulty of verbal communication.

That is a needlessly mathematical way to put something that is perfectly obvious. The problem remains, however. What are people supposed to do with those first nine months, or year and a half, when the language and your soft palate refuse to cooperate with one another? Why do you insist on aspirating your retroflex consonants at all of the wrong moments?

Well, that early period is one of anguish, even for "big" personalities, and as excruciating as a sunburn under wool clothes for shy people who never like to stand out in a crowd. It stands there like adolescence does between the likeable ten-year-old and the recovered twenty-year-old, an ugly period that has to be weathered. No one can do it for you. Money or smiles cannot purchase a short cut.

Language acquisition has nothing to do with raw, baseline intelligence; at least I like to tell myself this. It is, however, affected by age to a degree. Toddlers plow effortlessly through language like salmon do streams on their way back to the spawning grounds. Older fish find the stuff more viscous.

Other than by age, the Fates distribute their gifts with feckless irresponsibility. Knowing that, however, does not prevent missionaries from envying one another's random talents. It was always hard to speak Basha with even the most understanding Dhurgastani; it was downright impossible to speak Basha if another missionary was within earshot.

Do not compare yourself with others.

Do your best.

Go at your own speed.

We could all recite Kesab's language school prep talk; but that recitation did not keep me from being angry at Mary Syme for the language tripping so effortlessly on her lips. It had been easy for her from the first instant. The first day when we were memorizing "emergency texts," she had needed to hear it only once while the rest of us giggled at our inability. No matter how many more hours of drill I did than she, I bumbled along as she raced on through the lessons, finally disappearing over the horizon behind some obscure declension which I would never bother to learn.

People wonder if lay missionaries such as myself do evangelism, or are they too busy with secular work to remember the spiritual aspect of their responsibilities?

The question is rhetorical if one cannot speak the local language. One zealous group of young short-term outreach workers found us older, more long-term ones lacking. We were not involved enough in passing out tracts; we were, in their eyes, too busy. A short-term visitor with our Mission hitched a ride with members of one such outreach team. She had to listen to criticism of us as they wound through the hills, criticism which she knew to be largely unjustified. Having taken as much abuse of her friends as she could, she finished the conversation with a question, "But does your team know Basha?"

They did not. Their zeal did not allow for something as slow an investment as language learning.

Their criticism, nevertheless, should be heard. Much social gospel is really a good intention hidden behind bashfulness over poor language skills. If a nurse, for example, is an excellent nurse but has trouble understanding what is said to her in conversation, it is a natural instinct to throw herself into her nursing; it makes her feel better about not having discussions about her faith.

The easy route is to stay in one's office at headquarters, where the staff can all operate in English anyway, to hide behind a computer and produce great heaping reams of learned paperwork. The difficult route is to be out embarrassing yourself with your atrocious accent.

Sure, we all meant to get straight into theological

vocabulary, but it is a strange situation to be in when a person is able to discuss mankind's total depravity, and yet cannot politely ask if Aunt Bindhu is recovered from her fever. After how many years of living in California does a Vietnamese refugee learn the usage of words such as grace and justification?

It is no easier for the missionary. We learn at different paces. We only learn well what we frequently use. We only learn when we are forced into it by desperation. One of Kesab's gems went: "You have to murder a language before you can use it properly."

Bailiff:	All rise.
Judge:	Ladies and gentlemen of the jury, you have heard the evidence against the accused, have you reached a verdict?
Foreman:	We have, Your Honor.
Judge:	And what is your verdict?
Foreman:	Your Honor, we find the accused, Martin, guilty of murdering the language.

And multiple counts as well, I'm sure. I can merely plead innocent to its having been premeditated; but, in this case, that does not make a tremendous difference.

Not all mistakes are created equal, of course. Some are more dramatic than others, some are chronic, some seemed designed by the language's architect to trip me up. The Basha word for "dog" and that for "chicken" differ by a slim hair's breadth. It is embarrassing for a village when its animal doctor is continually going to farms in order to purchase "dog eggs." The word for "goat" was *bakra* and the word for "barn" was *goat*. Imagine how I fared when pushed for time and having to teach about proper housing for a goat flock. I was constantly building good goats so that my barns stayed warm and dry and did not catch pneumonia.

My farmers' classes were forgiving. I saved my worst blunders for the village church. Praying aloud in a group is intimidating to some people, but doing it in a new language is intimidating to anyone. When we had been around long enough for the kindly pastor to turn to me and sweetly ask for me to close the meeting with a word of prayer, the trouble began. Up until that fateful moment I had contented myself with fervent amens, a word both English and Basha have borrowed from Hebrew. I stumbled through that first time. It was the unprepared, impromptu part of the praying that was so death-defying. If only I could pray about vaccination of livestock or deworming sheep, these I could manage without a moment's hesitation.

I am not a child of a liturgical church; but memorized prayer was what was called for in this situation. I memorized Psalm 23, an appropriate sentiment and safe for any occasion, I reckoned.

Weeks passed. It took quite some time for the pastor to forget my last disappointing performance; but my chance did finally arrive: "Dr. Martin, would you please close us with a brief word of prayer?"

Aha, happy to!

I thought it went rather well. Those Dhurgastani who knew the psalm were impressed; those that did not would consider me something of a poet. The missionaries would do me homage as a model colleague.

It was not until later over coffee that a friend from Britain, no doubt to keep me from the sin of pride and conceit, broke it to me that I was suffering from some confusion in the use of the Basha suffix *lai*. It functions to identify the object of the sentence, to show who has the whatever done to it, as it were.

I thanked him, remembering the Proverb about "Correct a wise man and he will love thee," then went through the psalm in my head and realized that this *lai* thing was a powerful gadget. My prayer had run something like this:

> I am the Lord's shepherd,
> I shall not want.
> I make him to lie down in green pastures;
> I lead him beside the still waters . . .

Not exactly my intention, nor particularly edifying. But I am afraid to admit that even this blasphemy does not rank as my worst moment in three years brimming over with awful bloopers.

Later, I began teaching a youth Bible study on Tuesday evenings. The "youth" of our village congregation meant anyone between eight and fifty years in age and unmarried. We blasted through the highlights of the Old Testament in about six months, and that was fine. When I ran into shallow language skills, one of the university students with English could tow me back out to sea.

The problem came when we moved into the gospels. I was teaching the New Testament at night, while during the day I was lecturing on reproductive physiology. How can I put this discreetly? Suffice it to say that the Basha for "Apostle John" and for "vagina" are frightfully close. My daytime students were confused and my nighttime ones frequently scandalized. A ghastly mistake to make in a room full of teenagers.

February 28
Dear Folks,

Warm, sunny Saturday afternoon, very lazy. Joanne is

upstairs sleeping while I write on the stoop, surrounded by children with runny noses. Goats are staked out grazing. Didi (the generic word for older sister meaning any woman older than yourself) from next door sweeps out the ducks' pen. Though I can't see her, I'm confident that she is glaring at me as usual. She is a tough old nut to crack, and thus far I haven't impressed her. It did help my cause slightly this week when two American photojournalists came along to film Joanne and me. I suppose it made us appear important. At one point, while the video camera was running along, who should appear but Didi, dressed in her most splendid finery. She came over and squeezed herself in between Bijou and me; sat herself down very dignified—Dhurgastani gentry written all over her harsh face.

Language is going rough; but now as we have learned to use the past tense my sentences become more interesting. Knowing only the present tense brought new meaning to Jesus' words about living in the present and allowing each day to take care of its own problems. "Tense" has also taken on new meaning. Both past and present make me "tense."

I speak slowly, making sentences like glaciers make farmland. . . .

Gaining trust

Som Prasad was a Brahman farmer that I met in Katihar, in eastern Dhurgastan. He was a quiet man, especially for a Brahman, and had not said a word during our two-week-long course on animal health. But as I so often found, the quiet farmer that I assumed stupid was actually the best at any hands-on application of our material.

In Katihar we ran a month's vaccination program against

hemorrhagic septicemia, a devastating bacterial disease that can kill a water buffalo within short hours of the first symptoms. There had been an outbreak in nearby Umbu and that made for an ideal situation to raise the area's awareness of the Mission's animal health work.

We had trained Som and other farmers in the Katihar area to treat and to vaccinate against H.S. The villagers, however, had not used the services of our trainees. After questioning people I realized that one major reason for this disappointing situation was that people were not aware of who in their area had been sent to Bhadrapur for the training course. What we lacked was an effective advertising campaign, and this outbreak was our chance.

I arranged with the government for several thousand doses of vaccine to be flown to the area. Community health workers at the Mission hospital publicized the campaign. Then the trainees from every village did the actual vaccinating. I was there to reassure animal owners about what we were doing, and to keep an eye out for reactions to the vaccine. If only one animal were to go into shock and die from the crude vaccine, the whole month would become misadvertising.

The first day went slowly; the fellows had not found their rhythm yet. Ropes broke and sent my farmers crashing down hillsides followed by indignant livestock. I showed them how to better divide the labor: two handlers to truss up any hesitant buffalo, a record keeper/money collector and a syringe cleaner/vaccine giver. Things began to pick up.

As we went to a neighboring village, suddenly no one was interested in our services. This was disconcerting; the villagers insisted that they did not need it. Someone had been through a few days earlier to handle the situation.

Oh, really? That made me angry. Why should the government guys come out when they knew . . .

It was not the government.

With my language problems it took awhile to comprehend the situation. Evidently an industrious witch doctor had come through and sold insurance against the H.S. And sure enough, I began to notice that all of the buffalo and oxen in the village had violet-colored paint splashed about their horns as prevention.

Placebos work on psychosomatic illness among people, but people are sophisticated hypochondriacs. I am not convinced that positive thinking would have much impact with my patients and their problems.

I tried to reason it out with some elders without any luck. The paint, which had lasted ten days and was visible, was much more reassuring than my five cc's which simply disappeared beneath the animal's skin, never to be seen again. Seeing this stubborn cheapskate village's animals die might serve them right, but it would not bring me any joy.

At the next village I could see that the witch doctor had again beat us with his mark. Cattle stared out of the barns at me from between their violet horns, pleading with me to save them from their masters' ignorance.

I made a decision about which many of my supporters might not feel comfortable. I began to endorse the witch doctor. You could see the relief on the villagers' faces. They did not trust the foreigner's science, but they also hated to argue with it. Oh, I see. There's been a misunderstanding. Sure, it's fine to have the dye put on the horns; but didn't he tell you? No, I can see that he hasn't. The dye does not work unless the vaccine is given later. That's right. I winked at Som: Okay boys, rope her up!

The trainees thought that was a good one, sharp-dealing, and they were in on the joke.

The villagers consented but continued to be wary of the foreign innovation. Who knew what monstrous side effects it might bring?

Rumors abounded. A cow had aborted in the last village after receiving the shot. No, it was two buffalo that had aborted the day before yesterday. The reason for the noisy thunderstorm this morning was that this group of busy-bodies was going around sticking needles into cows. Of course, the gods were angry; it just made common sense when you treated sacred cows in such a casual, disrespectful way.

I followed up every rumor as best I could, but they were like echoes in a canyon, seeming to emanate from everywhere. Try to find out precisely which cow it was that aborted and it would all turn into mist.

A runner called to me from a hillside across the valley where we had worked that morning. The mayor of that last village had a prize Murrah buffalo imported from India, the finest animal in the entire district. The runner said that it was bloated now after being vaccinated.

I tried to act unperturbed for the benefit of the trainees. They would get so anxious over the smallest complication; but this was serious, an expensive animal belonging to an influential family. I grabbed antihistamine, epinephrine and a box of horrible ayurvedic herbal powder supposedly helpful in rumen tympany. Som wanted to accompany me, and we ran down the trail, across the valley and huffed up the hill to the runner. We set off together at a Dhurgastani pace, which in the hills is much too rapid for Westerners.

As we passed by houses, the danger to the prize buffalo grew. Wives called out to us from doorways. They had heard about her. She was no longer giving milk. She was in respiratory distress. She was down and could no longer rise to her feet. It kept getting worse, until I was jogging down the trail with my backpack pounding against me in encouragement. We reached the local school where the mayor was standing on a low wall haranguing a crowd of men about how my vaccine had killed his buffalo.

It must be true. We kept on going without stopping.

Oh Lord, surely you wouldn't let that one, of all animals, die? It would set back our work in this area for decades. No one would ever again trust Som and the other workers. It was bad enough for me, but I could go back to Bhadrapur and forget the whole thing; poor Som Prasad had to live here.

The trailside telegraph murmured that the Mission was going to have to buy the dead buffalo. I ran along the trail that, four hours earlier in the chilly morning, I had been nervous to even creep along. Down a steep slope, through another clump of houses, jumping down the fields from terrace to terrace. We could see the mayor's large house standing accusingly on the shoulder of a barren hill. The barn was behind the house.

I turned the corner trying to steel myself for whatever it would reveal; and there stood the ugly black brute, chewing her cud contentedly. No bloat, no death, no symptoms. She was healthy enough, in fact, that Som and I could not get near enough to give her any of the medicines that she did not need. The mayor's wife was surprised to see us again so soon. Why no, her buffalo was not sick; should it be? Would we care for a cup of tea?

Som and I walked the two hours back to where we had left the rest of the group. In my relief, I did not bother to question the runner. When we passed the schoolyard again, it was deserted. The trailside telegraph was quiet, closed for the afternoon.

My language was never sufficient to uproot these pernicious rumors or to be absolutely confident that I could afford to neglect them. To ignore one valid problem was to court real complications.

Som had become a cowboy in the course of our past three weeks together. No sooner did the others have a frothing monster roped up than Som was in and out with the subcutaneous injection. The first day of working he had broken four of my plastic syringes. I had brought only ten for the entire month and lay in bed sweating that night over the possibility of calling off the whole program after two and a half days because I had not brought enough syringes. He learned, however, how to stop breaking them, giving the injection in three distinct steps: plant the needle up to its hub in a fold of skin (the animal leaps), attach the syringe to the needle in one deft motion (the animal leaps again), blast the medicine in. The trick was pausing and not fighting with the creature at the two points when it invariably tried to get airborne.

In the midst of the tussles, as blood and horns and manure flew in every direction, Som and I built a camaraderie. He did not, however, speak to me. Perhaps he was embarrassed that his mentor had a vocabulary small enough to shame a five-year-old. I could understand Som as he spoke to the others through the yellow scarf that he always wore wrapped around his face and over his mouth; but when he turned to me, he restricted himself to hand signals. He could not understand when I spoke because he had decided that he could not understand. After I finished, he would turn to the others and ask for a translation. I cannot imagine how he managed to learn anything from me during the training course in Bhadrapur.

Old village women pulled the same maddening routine. I would ask a question in what I had been told was a respectable Basha accent, and it might as well have been Swahili for all that it accomplished. What did he say? Did you understand what he said, because I didn't? How can he treat my oxen when he can't talk properly?

She had probably never spoken to someone whom she did not know before.

The problem of accents and dialects

Sitting on a sunny porch one afternoon, resting after a weary hike, I noticed a woman watching me intently. Missionaries are accustomed to causing a sensation everywhere they go, no matter how routine a thing they may be doing. But this woman's stare was noticeable even to someone used to being a freak.

A Dhurgastani colleague noticed as well. "Have you ever seen a man like that before?" he asked, smiling. She shook her head no.

It took me a moment. I was the tallest thing in any crowd I happened to join; I wore funny clothes. Then I realized that they meant a Caucasian. She had never seen a foreigner previously. She had never heard Basha spoken with an American accent. She quite probably had never guessed the existence of other languages.

Farmers have their own separate vocabulary when it comes to diseases. It is that way in every country. Veterinarians learn all of the polysyllabic Latin terminology in school and anger their clients should they ever forget themselves and speak that way in an examination room. Keep it simple, Doc.

Stagnation at lungs equals pneumonia; blue-bag is mastitis; lumpy jaw is actinomycosis.

The professional vocabulary that I was so excited to receive in Rajdhani was frequently useless out in the hills. That's all right. I'll just learn the colloquial expressions.

It is not that easy. In a country like Dhurgastan, crossing from one valley to another can mean a change in dialects. I learned a word for liver fluke—our most common animal health problem in the hills—and I felt like I had accomplished something great. Only it did not work up the river in Chhindwari. Was it my pronunciation? Was I using the wrong "t"? (Basha has four "t"s, each pronounced differently.)

No, it was the wrong word. One hour away, through a pleasant bit of jungle and along the irrigation canal, across a bridge—and they used a different word for the most common livestock disease.

So, I had two words for fluke and felt myself an authority and well-prepared. Wouldn't old Kesab smile to see me going beyond the call of duty?

But there was Katihar and Umbu, Shujabad and Bhind. I learned five words for liver fluke, and since a given animal health course might include farmers from several districts, my lecture on the life cycle of *fasciola* had to include them all. Someone always was confused and left out. I tried all five of my words to no effect. His neighbors would chime in to help; still no bells ringing. Then a glimmer of suspicion would appear; you could see them working up to a tentative attempt. "Liver fluke?" they would ask in English.

I came to expect that sort of thing. If, as I was reading in Basha script for my language teacher and I came to a word that stopped me dead, a terrible combination of rarely used letters, it was routinely an English word transliterated.

Language problems came wrapped in surprising packages that had never occurred to me. There was the oxen driver at the farm in Bhadrapur, a spindly, dark and murderous-looking individual. The oxen, however, were not put off by his appearance and adored him. I named the two beasts "Lazy" and "Greedy"; and they would not cooperate with anyone but their usual driver. If he was absent on the day when we demonstrated to farmers how to cast a large bullock with only the use of twelve meters of rope, what was with him a pleasant lesson, without him turned into a battle of minds.

The driver had a severely cleft lip and palate. In America this would have either been repaired while he was a child or have been considered a tremendous disfigurement. In Dhurgastan there was a shrug, "These things happen," and acceptance.

In fact, he put his malformation at the service of his devious sense of humor. At serious moments, when I was concentrating on something else, the driver would catch my eye and stick his tongue out of one of his broad nostrils. It was hideous and I rewarded him with a hysterical reaction the first time that he tried it out on me. He knew I disliked it and held it in reserve for when he wanted to really irritate me.

The deformity also rendered his speech almost entirely unintelligible to me.

As acting manager of the farm all disputes and delicate personnel matters sooner or later were seated in front of me to see justice done. Matters that would have caused Solomon to retire from the bench, I blundered into with my poor Basha, and my even worse understanding of Asian ways of dealing with things. I was always trying the direct approach and causing innocents to suffer more than they needed to.

I cudgeled through situations that required surgical tweezers, but I managed. With everyone, that is, except the oxen driver. He frequently needed to speak with me, and with his Brahman sense of his own importance, the talking always had to be done alone, discreetly in my office. There was no chance of having another person to attend and help me in my decision, to help me understand what he was talking about. There was that time about birth control and his wife's fertility, that one about his fisticuffs with my clinic technician outside of farm hours, the loan for something or other. He would speak in hushed tones for long minutes, his eyes expressing that it was most urgent. I learned that it did no good to ask him to repeat a word that I had not caught; there were too many of them. I listened, then pulled myself to full height in my chair and delivered my decision as they knew how to in the empire of the Medes and Persians. "Thus have I spoken; thus let it be done."

There is no telling if the problems that I solved for the oxen driver were the ones that he had approached me about.

June 27
Dear Folks,

Last Sunday we had our oral language tests. They bring in a Dhurgastani language instructor from another school who must endure thirty minutes with each of my classmates as we fumble through our nouns and trip over our verbs. He must have done something particularly heinous to deserve such a fate.

Examiner:	Why did you come to Dhurgastan?
Student:	(intended answer) I came to serve the people.
Student:	(actual answer) I came to smell the people.

If the Persian Gulf war had not been a hot number at the moment, I feel sure that my own international incident would have received more press attention. Oh well, they graduated us and are sending us on to Bhadrapur anyway. . . .

CHAPTER 5

Habitual Fender-Benders

When Cultures Collide

"Everyday, from here to there, funny things are everywhere."

Dr. Seuss

Cultures handle life's little difficulties differently. That is one of the things that makes cultures different. Simple; we all knew that. Aha, the nasty surprises lie like land mines on the borders between cultures. Silent, no one really knows where they are; if we did, it would be an easy matter to merely step around them. Sagacious men avoid the area, but the job of a missionary is to cross the border even though it lies across a mine field.

"Are you planning on having children? How big a family do you hope for?"

Harmless questions to ask a married couple of child-bearing years. Small talk, easy openers, nothing particularly intimate. To American couples.

As it is, however, you have placed a careless boot down and put your full weight upon it. Kaboom. One evening blown to smithereens.

Joanne and I routinely offended Dutch friends with our seemingly innocuous questions. Our view was that a couple not taking active steps to prevent conceiving children was a couple planning on having a family. To a good Dutch Calvinist, such questions toyed with the blasphemous and were an insult to God's sovereign control over all events. The Dutch, ordinarily forceful and forthright, required kid gloves on the subject. It was so out of the national character that I never guessed, and we went on for months, blithely stepping on people's sensitivities. Many casualties later, a Dutch friend who had become close enough to trade in intimacies broke it to me. We had been hairy awful barbarians without it ever occurring to us.

Kaboom. Nasty surprise.

People are the same wherever you go. Simple, we all knew that.

Every person, regardless of race, creed, sex, religion, nationality, inherent intelligence and dental records is a frothy mixture of virtue and selfish egotism. Everyone intentionally violates what they know of morality. As a stamp collector I have noticed how many stamps, in assorted colors and designs, the United States has printed with the word "Love" upon them. These are to make us feel friendly and compassionate. No culture could argue against love, though they may have different things in mind as they postmark it. However, I have never seen a U.S. stamp centered around a theme of "goodness." That is a troubling word. It is harder to reach a consensus about; it is not particularly popular (nor ever has been). Worst of all, it is unobtainable even were we to get serious about the obtaining. In the sight of God, all men of all tribes are sinners. Whether there are degrees of sin worth distinguishing is a question that I will leave others to debate.

Every culture faces many of the same basic problems, regardless of its millennium or relative development. If the tribe or city-state or nation is to grow, it must have children. There is, therefore, the question of what is going to comprise a family, how it shall be organized and established. Families may be monogamous, polygamous, patriarchal or matriarchal. Marriages may be arranged by parents, hired professionals or the couples themselves. But families there shall be; and if families, then children to be raised and educated. By whom? About what?

All civilizations evolve customs about eating and toiletry, hospitality, greeting and conversation. Peoples and people are at the deepest, taproot level alarmingly similar no matter which continent their ancestors happened to conquer. Culture is made up of the various ingenious answers dreamed up to answer the unavoidable questions of social existence. The awful wonder of history is that we do not feel drawn to one another by our root similarities, but rather despise and suspect each other over the cosmetic differences.

Joanne was a young woman, new to Dhurgastan and a little edgy. She traveled across Rajdhani alone one day in the back of a taxi. A pair of dark eyes looked at her from the rear-view mirror.

"So, how old are you?" asked the eyes when they learned that Joanne could speak some Basha. "Are you married?"

She considered having him stop and let her out on a busy sidewalk, but instead pled bad language comprehension.

This perfectly respectable Dhurgastani banter held all sorts of threats of hidden meaning to someone from the sex-sick West.

As a man I was asked less about family matters and more about how much money I made each month. Poor as my salary was, it could rival a Dhurgastani executive, had there been any such thing. One learned to answer without answering. "Enough." "About half of what I would be making had I stayed in my own country."

There was the morning that the meterman came to our village to read the electric company's meters. The usual group of neighbors was sitting on the green in front of our house, with their knees against their chests, smoking cigarettes and talking about the price of buffalo. One of these fellows called out to the meterman next door, "Hey, how much was their bill?" There resounded a loud reply of an enormous amount of rupees. "For one month?" the group buzzed incredulously like excited insects.

No Right of Privacy Act; perfectly fair and in-bounds. All completely normal to them; all completely embarrassing to me.

Kaboom. Nasty surprise in reverse.

Other land mines

It is only these cultural differences and an unfamiliar language that render foreign missions foreign. Living conditions can be strange, and the climate may be new to one, but these obstacles are only changes of degree. A minister from small-town Alabama who took a pastorate in urban Boston would almost rank as a foreign missionary; both he and the parishioners would recognize that.

The Rural Development Institute to which I was assigned had a business manager from Finland. Prior to coming to Dhurgastan, Liisa had done accounting for the municipal government of a little country village. She was in language school with us, but that experience was even more harrying for her. Not only must she master Basha; she had to do so using the vehicle of English. She had to spend several months in Britain studying English before she could come to Asia and settle down to a plateful of Basha.

Dhurgastan was foreign to both Liisa and me; and though

we had the Reformation in common, we were quite foreign to each other as well.

One bright morning I rode the farm motorcycle down the hill from the farm and into the big RDI offices. Liisa was disconcerted when I walked unannounced into her office, clasped my hands in front of me with the elbows pointed outward and broke into "Some Enchanted Evening." She was busy going through records with a Dhurgastani auditor hired by the Mission to keep us honest. Her eyebrows took on that angle which I knew meant that she was not fully appreciative of the performance.

My finale completed, she asked in husky politeness if I might grace her with an explanation of my behavior. With that question she fell into my trap, and I placed before her one of her little blue and white memos. These normally caused me great alarm when I found one in my mail slot because they ordinarily meant that I had made yet another business mistake that would take a day and a half locked in my office with the file cabinet to get straight.

Liisa had written this one to me two days previously:

> Please come at your convenience to my office. I need
> you to come in and sing something.

She had of course meant "sign something."

Finns are so fair-skinned they are almost translucent, but it gives them the ability to blush dramatically. And Liisa looked like a tropical sunrise.

In an interdenominational Mission that included people from more than twenty nations, we had as many cultural exchanges among ourselves as with the Dhurgastanis. These were rarely painful, however, and almost uniformly enriching. Efficiency was an entirely different matter.

Initial messages on a subject were commonly mis-
construed, causing what one had foolishly expected to be
a small transaction to blossom into major logistical
problems. If our mission is even roughly analogous to the
efficiency of NATO, then President Yeltsin could be in Paris
with his army on any given afternoon that suited him.

Dear Friends,

A tall thin man came to the farm one dewy Saturday
morning and said that his buffalo could not calf; that,
at least is what I heard, *byaune*. What he actually said
was *byaugute*, a rip roaring bacterial infection in cattle
and buffalo that causes a high fever. Then the animal's
throat swells to such proportions that the victim can
asphyxiate in eight short hours from onset of
symptoms. Even the least medical of you realize that the
treatment of the two conditions is fundamentally different.

But I was still new to Dhurgastan and had not yet
learned about *byaugute*. My farm staff assumed that the
doctor knew what he was dealing with.

We walked four hours to his village, leaving the road,
crossing the river and then up into a pass hidden in
thunderclouds. Alternately we roasted on the hillsides,
lugging all of my calving gear, and then shivered
through a chilly rain.

I was winded when we arrived; but immediately set
to work on the situation, trying with an icy calm to
show the gathering crowd that they had found the right
man for the job, one who really knew what he was
about.

These crowds were something that I had to come to
terms with during my first months practicing in Asia.

One had to appropriate the bedside manner of a traveling salesman; good work was not enough, it needed to be good entertainment. There wasn't much else playing that cloudy Saturday afternoon up high in the little Gurung village.

I blew up a shoulder length plastic glove, the better to stick my arm in it easily, and this simple action caused quite a sensation in my audience. I soaped myself up and was ready to deliver the little rascal.

I try not to consider what that crowd must have thought as they watched me examine the buffalo per rectum and discover to my consternation no sign of imminent birth, much less a calf.

Our great diagnostician had, however, during the course of his examination noticed that the patient felt terribly hot. She had almost cooked my arm. Her temperature sent the mercury crashing to the farthest end of my thermometer.

Once again (or so I thought) led astray by an owner's mistaken history.

I now began doing all of those things that one is always supposed to do. I looked at the whole creature and noticed that she was breathing with difficulty and that her throat, just at the larynx was oddly swollen and hard to the touch.

I scratched my head, puzzled, and told the family (who looked equally as confused but for their own reasons) that she was not ready to calf, but I thought that she could do with a great, heaping, massive dose of antibiotics . . . (what was the Basha for antibiotics, anyway?). She needed a shot for her fever.

No one dared to correct this confident foreign expert. They made the same error as my farm staff and assumed that what looked to them as idiocy was, in fact, Western genius and know-how.

After giving the injection I trudged home, giving out a Bible to a university student on the trail who asked for English reading material. Weeks later, I learned the word for that dratted disease and realized what had happened to me on that monsoon Saturday. Needless to say, I have not been called back to help improve the quality of animal health in that particular village. I am only thankful that I had not been dealing with a buffalo bull.

Unsolicited Philosophizing: The Apostle Paul put it this way: ". . . this mere outward show—and the world around you is nothing more—is fast fleeting away." If that is true—and I firmly believe it is—may God grant us the common sense to live for what is not illusion and for that which is everlasting.

Your partner,
Martin

Cultural and denominational quirks

Foreign missions has received a lot of bad press for its reputation of bringing with the gospel of Jesus its own homeland's cultural foibles and petty denominational squabbles, of putting African natives into tweed suits and brassieres. I can comment upon only my own experience, not that of the history of missions as a whole; but for my part, I saw no evidence of these unintentional imports. Foreign aid workers, so critical of mission policies, seemed more guilty of bringing in their luggage, cultural idiosyncrasies best left at home. Granted, I am more than likely blind to my own faults.

In Dhurgastan we were protected from ourselves in many ways due to the government's ban on all proselytizing. Opposition to the Church drove the missionaries together into one organization; we were not, therefore, present as Anglicans, Baptists, Lutherans, Methodists and Presbyterians. At home these people would have first drawn swords and then drawn blood, but in Dhurgastan's pressure they worked and worshiped together most amiably.

We were not more sanctified than the varied agencies that sent us; it was more as if our swords were taken from us at the border. The Dhurgastani Church explains our unusual tolerance, because its indigenous leadership was responsible to decide those issues that ordinarily would have divided us. They decided when baptism was to take place, how communion was to be served, what were to be the order and methods of worship. Had the missionaries desired to have theological arguments with one another, they would have first had to run roughshod over the Dhurgastani believer. We functioned to supplement the local church with our talents, to help put into practice the plans of local leadership.

A good missionary lives under a constant low level of unseen tension, like the small stray current that flowed through our refrigerator. Joanne could only register it when she was barefooted. It is not at all popular to admit, but the fact is that the goal of missions does include changing the prevailing local culture. This sounds scandalizing, paternalistic, crude and dogmatic. At least one misconception, however, can be quickly made to "walk the plank." The change is not to be Westernizing, much less Americanizing. I am no friend of Eastern thought; but the gospel, if accepted, will act very ungentlemanly. It has broad ramifications, and, without knocking, marches into the halls of government, ethics and education. Jesus, and therefore His Church, has much to say on family values, on how women are treated; and it is no good pretending it is not so in order to be accepted by secular anthropologies.

Christianity, real truth, refuses to remain docile on a quiet library shelf, between 900 and 910 of the Dewey Decimal System. This is not the ground surrounding Golgotha.

We do not offer a more aesthetic, more successful religion to replace a primitive, outmoded one. This is not a case of the steam engine replacing the mule; this is the blind being made to see. If a blind person were to suddenly gain his sight, chances are he is going to repaint that apartment and shuffle the furniture around.

It is emphatically not the business of the missionary to change superficial customs which happen to rankle those of his own culture. For example, in Dhurgastan good breeding dictates that one never step over any part of another person. The bottom of a foot is considered disgustingly impure (not so far from the truth in a land with so few toilets), and to step over a person is to point the bottom of your foot at them, a sign of extreme contempt.

I should imagine that Christianity will have no comment to make on this particular custom. The British probably asked pardon after belching when they were still un-catechized Celts; the Church's emissaries left them to continue in the inexplicable practice. The Dhurgastani custom, however, does cause the Christians quite some inconvenience. Meetings at the church are often crowded and floor space is at as much of a premium as Manhattan office space. Men and women are required to sit on opposite sides of the floor, and it can be a hilarious feat of balancing to weave one's way to a vacant spot without severely insulting several others. People come late anyway, so a sermon is interrupted many times to allow the crowd to shift and absorb a late arrival.

The Church, with a few tenacious exceptions, decided long, long, ago that Sunday was the proper Christian sabbath, a break from the old Hebrew tradition of a Saturday sabbath. Dhurgastan's weekly holiday is Saturday and so for pragmatic rather than theological reasons, that is the day on which congregations gather. Should missionaries insist on a change and make the church come into line with universal practice?

"Of course not," everyone answers in unison. That would be a senseless change of format without enough substance to warrant the difficulties. Tradition, however, will not go away until it has had the last word; and though the church meets together on Saturday, the children leave the service halfway through and attend what is known as Sunday school. Some future church historian shall, no doubt, find this as evidence of synchretism between pagan Hinduism and the early Dhurgastani church. "As can be clearly seen by this evidence the new converts still wanted to cling to their old customs of worshiping the elements, at this date restricted to sun worship."

Culture and hospitality

The Dhurgastani people are hospitable to a fault. Guests eat first and are offered second and third portions even if this leaves nothing for the rest of the family. As a guest, you have to get forceful with a hostess to convince her that another serving of rice is not your secret desire. You do this by throwing yourself over your plate, like a brave marine might do a live hand grenade, physically preventing the ladle from delivering more food.

It is a social ballet, the steps of which one must learn. If a coy space is left open by your hands, the hostess' job is to deftly manage to slip more lentils onto the steaming plate, while the guest's job is vainly to protest and then gladly to eat it all.

Needless hassle? Perhaps, but one might argue that such things keep life from being strictly utilitarian. Table manners in the southern United States are not altogether very different. A Texan hostess will ask her guests if they would not care for another portion. The polite guest refuses diffidently and will not accept more food until she persists a third time. I have almost starved to death visiting friends in Maryland who for some unknown reason took a person's yes for yes, and his no for no.

While following up on our village animal health workers in remote locations, I was subject to local hospitality, and one night I was staying with a kind family. The weather was hot and muggy, and the kitchen in which we squatted while eating was filled with smoke. I was not very hungry. This was my second night with this household, so I was prepared for the struggle ahead and firmly resolved to refuse seconds.

My wizened hostess was, however, a sharp one, a virtuoso. She had been performing this ballet before I was born. She swooped down upon my unguarded plate with a great slab of sticky rice before I could stop her. The guest, once bested, cannot protest too hotly, or else the message is interpreted that the food is not tasty. I, therefore, smiled angelically, but I had learned her method.

Dhurgastan is one of those societies which differentiates between the work of the left and of the right hand. The right hand is clean and ceremonially pure while the left is reserved for more necessary, but less mentionable, duties. My left hand by necessity and social convention lay dead and lifeless at my side as I ate, and when I took rice and lentils to my mouth with the right one (eating utensils not being used), the old bird would zoom in with her ladle.

Presto, another direct hit.

She did it with such finesse, without seeming to even notice if my plate was getting empty. I ate slowly, trying to show that my appetite was not its usual self. As my right hand made another trip mouthward, the great full ladle began another bombing run.

I could not help myself; it was reaction born of decades of ambidextrous eating. My left hand leapt up from its slumbers and sought to cover my dish, but the blocking motion was a nanosecond too slow and that hand ever so slightly grazed the bowl of the ladle.

My hostess never changed her expression. The great ballerina picked herself up after having been dropped by an amateur colleague. Without a pause, but as if it had all along been her intention, she laid aside the defiled instrument and spent the rest of the meal wrestling with her enormous cooking pot, hefting it over the dinner plates and pouring out its bubbling contents.

Living with a Dhurgastani family during language school had the advantage that we lost the gleam of guests and became regulars at dinner. Our time in that house did expose us to a life not seen from the passing tourist buses.

CHAPTER 6

The Forty-Hour Missionary

Working Overseas

"Doing good without God is diabolical."

Dostoevski

Dear Friends,

A busy month: I taught the last of this winter's animal health courses. My colleague from Scotland left Dhurgastan for furlough, but an American vet with the Peace Corps stopped in for ten days to help me teach.

So what will I do when not teaching the courses, you ask? *If you can't do one thing well, be so busy no one will dare mention it!*

People are more important than programs. I'm committed to that view, but it is easy to forget. When one gets caught up with the AC (Advisory Committee), the PMC (Planning and Management Committee), the ECC (Extended Coordinating Council), the urgent correspondence to answer, one forgets that the grass cutting lady is more significant than them all.

Nevertheless, I thought that those supporting our work and making it possible deserved a brief list of our involvements here at the farm now that the season's courses were finished.

- Clinic: We, of course, treat local animals seven days a week.

- Drug Sales: We provide veterinary medicines for several remote projects. I suppose that this makes me a "pusher."

- Program Evaluation: Plans are to interview farmers and their neighbors in several far-flung villages in order to see if the efforts of the past ten years have been successful and what things we need to change.

- Saanen Goat Trial: Although this sounds like the Scope's Monkey Trial, what we are actually doing is determining if a particular breed of milk goat is appropriate for Dhurgastan.

- Grass Demonstration Plots: Many people wander through our farm, and we are trying to acquaint them with new types of available pasture grasses.

- Kudzu Trial: This is not a Stephen King horror novel. Instead, it is an attempt to see if this legume works well in raising rabbits.

- Video: We are filming the story of one of our village animal health workers to be used to encourage our other trainees. I have been told by someone from the Bombay film industry that I am a terrific director but a lousy cameraman.

- Tuberculosis Study: You'll hear more about this in coming months. I am convinced that animals here play an important part in this disease so rampant among the human population.

- Textbook: After ten years, the program is publishing its materials so that others may use them.

It Splices, Dices and Makes Millions of Julienne Fries:
And there remain other projects with intriguing

names which we are doing with various degrees of success: Alley Cropping, Live Fencing, Ginger under Trees (a second-rate Gothic love story), Flashcards on Breeding Stock Selection, a paper for the Pakribas Agricultural Institute, Bee Husbandry. . . . As you can see, our wee program is a publishing and film industry titan in the making. Move over George Lucas and Rupert Murdock.

I surely don't list these things to impress you, but as partners you're entitled to know what the firm is up to. I listed these diverse things as if I alone am responsible. This, of course, is not true. There is a cast of . . . well, a couple of other folks anyway.

Another Philosophical Friday Night:

The "Problem of Evil" has now boiled down for me into its most essential elements and might better be retitled the "Problem of Nasal Leeches."

Rats, snakes, spiders, blood and gore—I reckon I've seen it all, and I thought I was beyond being flustered. Not so. Nasal leeches give me the heebie-jeebies.

The poor old dog showed up at the back of our classroom looking sheepish and embarrassed. A good-natured mutt with a chronic dry cough and a blood-tinged nasal discharge. The owner thought that it was a nasal leech, but I discounted the diagnosis. It's the middle of the dry season. But to appease the woman I offered water to the dog and would not let him drink. Sure enough, the tip of an ugly brown tentacle emerged at the left nostril; the leech wanted to drink. He was a perniciously wary rascal and would always zip back out of reach whenever I tried to snatch him with a pair of forceps.

Well, I'll spare you most of the gruesome details that

followed, of the hours I spent watching that nose like a patient fisherman on a frozen lake staring at the hole he has made in the ice. We tried all of the recommended remedies: tobacco juice to cause the poor brute to sneeze explosively, chloroform spirits, salt water. Even this even-tempered canine was beginning to get irritated with us. I took him home and anesthetized him, thinking that perhaps the leech would relax as well. No luck.

A dose of Ivermectin of course would do to this horror about like kryptonite would to Superman; but, of course, Ivermectin is not available in Dhurgastan, and we try to limit ourselves to those medicines that our trainees can obtain. I continued to wait and the next day finally caught hold of the creature and drug it writhing into the light of day.

Disgusting? Believe me, I know. Too bad for you that it happened on the day that I try to write our monthly letter to supporters. Not particularly edifying? I know. But most of missionary life is lived somewhere just short of the peak of Mount Zion.

Better Things Do Happen:

Our youth group is growing, and the kids seemed to enjoy our survey of the Old Testament. Joanne is involved in the organized hysteria that is our Sunday school program, and she is teaching English to a young village fellow. They have had some great discussions about why it is that Christians believe certain things.

Your partner,
Martin

The problem with job descriptions

A friend of mine was a philosophy major at Wheaton

College. He was considering foreign missions as a career and decided to spend a summer overseas to get a look at missionaries from close range. The summer program packed him off to India to do street evangelism. Things were admirably organized, and he was met by friendly people at the airport.

"Ah, our hospital administrator," beamed the head of the welcoming party.

"Um, no. I'm afraid there has been a mistake. I am the new street evangelist," corrected my friend.

The welcoming party exchanged knowing glances. "No mistake. You are the new hospital administrator."

My friend spent his summer in the office of a rural hospital in Northern India. A horror story? It could have been but was not necessarily. Once he adjusted to the radical shift in plans, he did valuable work and learned a summer full of valid lessons. If it is a horror story, then it is one replayed over and over again in missions work. It is, in fact a well-loved favorite. Trained, eager professionals are thrust into unforeseen circumstances, given responsibilities with which they are not comfortable, handed the keys to the store and wished good luck. My friend's time in India, doing something that he did not feel confident about, was in reality great preparation to serve as a missionary.

Someone with personnel duties in our own mission board once confided to me that he considered flexibility the single greatest requirement of a missions worker. He assumed, but left unspoken, the need of fervent devotion to God and a sincere drive to be obedient to His will. A candidate's application needed to evince a flexible, teachable attitude or he would do his best to see that it did not get past his desk. The tense and unyielding fracture when they are asked to accommodate to changing conditions, to perform jobs for which they were not formally prepared. If there is a task that is unavoidable, and should some inflexible person refuse to perform it, the work then falls onto some-one else in the team, someone more than likely equally as ill-prepared and even busier.

Our own unavoidable day arrived; and once again, as when we decided to come to Asia, our lives seemed to step out into the empty space over an abyss of unknown depth. It had not occurred to me that after the shock of initially arriving in Dhurgastan we would have to again stomach that awful sensation. I had thought that goodbyes to family and friends had taken care of our mandatory moment of anxiety. With the end of language school, however, it was off into our real projects. We awoke and remembered that we had not come in order to be professional language students. We remembered that the language basics were acquired in order to go out and work.

The trunks were once more packed; hard farewells said to our dear ones from language school. The safe harbor of the Mission guesthouse disappeared in the smoke and dust behind our bus.

I am a veterinarian. It is a good, honest, demanding profession. In the United States I worked in a practice that saw any kind of animal with two exceptions: we would not examine poisonous snakes or primates. The reason to abstain from the snakes is obvious; the interdiction against monkeys was for several reasons. They carry diseases com-municable to man; but more importantly, they are smart, fast and strong. Special knowledge is required, otherwise the animal or his attending physician are liable to get damaged.

Those two exceptions, however, left plenty of latitude to claim the title of general practitioner. There was the iguana, who after faring badly in a tussle with a house cat, needed an enema every ten days; the leopard with hypocalcemia because his foolish owner kept it on an all meat diet; the stable full of Dutch warm-blooded horses with feet the size of dinner plates. When it became known that I could see damaged wildlife, my office witnessed a steady parade of odd creatures and even odder clients. The wildlife was indigent, for the most part, but there was also the usual paying menagerie of dogs, cats, sheep and goats, cattle, gerbils, budgerigars and Hannibal, my favorite guinea pig.

Hannibal was a generous little rascal who used to bring me cigars when he visited. This was especially touching considering that I was responsible for his wife's death. She had needed an emergency Caesarian section, which I performed. She survived the surgery, remarkable considering our ignorance about anesthesia and anatomy in the species; but she died later in the recovery room. Her veterinarian had forgotten that guinea pigs have cheek pouches. Mrs. Hannibal aspirated a carrot sliver into her trachea. . . .

So I had reason to consider myself flexible, accomplished at flying into uncharted territory by the seat of my pants, the Charles Lindbergh of veterinary medicine.

The Mission tries its best to find the right person to fill a position, but there are numerous factors that make the task like a 10,000 piece jigsaw puzzle of a Jackson Pollack painting: sudden illness in staff, projects that last longer than terms of fieldworkers, thankless jobs that no one who could pass a psychological evaluation would truly want to do.

It gets complicated. A certain hectic project office manager's wife develops a crippling allergy to a pollen found throughout Dhurgastan. Medical people strongly recommend that the family return to their home or consider working for a mission in a different country. In any case, a new business manager is needed because his job is having to be done on a half-time basis by the project's tutorial group teacher, and the strain of trying to do two busy jobs is starting to show upon her. Normally so joyful a spirit, she now occasionally lashes out at people angrily. Fine. The Mission has other business people; let one of them go and fill the spot.

But a large component of the work is training Dhurgastani staff to take on parts of the task. Now we need someone who knows how to teach and can do so in reasonably fluent Basha. It is not a job for a recent arrival. Well, three or four of our business folks are old-timers and can probably manage. But there is a long history of personnel problems in the project. Four years ago there was a big strike, and it has only been the skills of the recent business manager that kept the office peaceful and functioning. They need someone as forceful and personable as he was. The profile of the perfect replacement grows more and more narrow.

Add to this that it is a rural project in a very hilly district. Only a person in good physical shape will survive—and that eliminates Hans-Olaf, otherwise the best candidate; but his knees give him trouble since his motorcycle accident. The project also depended on the departing fellow to help lead the village's Bible study, and the project director has written to ask if the new person could be a gifted Bible teacher as well.

The list goes on and on until no one person in the Mission can fulfill all of the desires of everyone. If the replacement enjoys teaching accounting but not the Pentateuch, this means that either someone else must fill the gap, or else the Wednesday Bible study must be chopped out of the weekly calendar. Someone has to be uprooted from one project in which he or she is a trusted asset and go fill the shoes of a departing favorite. The Dhurgastani staff is skeptical; the chemistry between the missionaries will change with the addition of a new ingredient. No matter what or who, everyone is in for a period of acclimating.

April 13

Dear Folks,

I do not know how to begin. This past week was work orientation, and they sent me out to Benni to get a taste of real hill country life among farmers who have taken our animal health course.

Benni is just a three hour bus ride and then an eight hour walk outside Rajdhani. Without exaggeration I can say that it was the most difficult week of my life thus far. It was not an auspicious beginning to one's missions career.

I have seen the "real Dhurgastan"—just a day's walk away, but three hundred years ago. Rugged, self-sufficient people toiling out their lives against the hardships of a rugged, uncaring landscape. They are ingenious at surviving in such an inhospitable land, and one cannot help but feel that those men and women out digging in those steep rocky fields are as much a part of the environment as the cliffs and dry stream beds.

There are very few machines and so the only sounds as we hiked along the trails were the wind and the high-pitched cries of the hawks.

This time of year only the river at the bottom of the valley is running, so in a household with three daughters, two of them spend four hours a day just making trips for the day's water supply. These girls, therefore, cannot go to school; they are needed at home, so only the boys attend. Erosion, landslides and deforestation are rampant; but these people exist so close to the edge of the brink, that the Mission workers in the area are hard put to convince them to try any new, foreign techniques.

We walked through an area that I was told had been a forest two weeks earlier; only felled trees remained in every direction. When the missionary leading me around for my orientation asked a family what had happened to the trees, they explained that a government survey team had entered the valley. This is a great tragedy and a good example of much in this country. Faced with rampant deforestation, the government tried nationalizing the forest stands several years ago. It was a terrible failure of a well-meant policy. Though discontinued, farmers still fell all of their trees rather than risk the government taking them away.

I met several characters worthy of Rudyard Kipling's imagination during my brief stay. One success story was Chundra Bahadur. He believed the advice given him by an old missionary and began planting seedlings on the local community grazing lands. His neighbors were so worried that the government would take the land that they uprooted the trees and threatened to kill Chundra. But he kept at it until the hillside around his own fields was no longer bare but lush in comparison. He also terraced his fields better to stop his topsoil from leaving down stream for India and planted a kitchen garden. He raised milk goats and rabbits as well. Somewhere along the line he became a Christian, the only known believer in the valley; and he had such a sweet spirit about him. In his example, it is impossible to divorce his acceptance of Christ's gospel and all of the improved agricultural techniques. In him the two seemed to go hand in hand; once a Christian, he was open to other changes and not bound to traditional farming methods, or to his neighbors' opinions.

The community has watched with growing interest how Chundra Bahadur has made himself a prosperous man. They have begun to listen to his advice about chickens. Maybe they will hear out his religious ideas also.

Another character was the night watchman at a forest nursery where we spent two nights. For the most part Dhurgastanis are a clean-cut group; a man with a beard is either an aged grandfather, a Moslem or a Communist agitator. This night watchman, however, had long black hair and a tangled, matted beard that accentuated his wide, roving eyes. He appeared a dangerous-looking individual. I had watched him during a farmer's meeting that we had held at the nursery. In order to keep things maintained, the Mission gives ownership of materials to individuals, and the blackboard belonged to the night watchman. It lived up to its name, being but a piece of plywood painted black. The night watchman guarded it as his most prized possession.

He had the mannerisms of a night creature, appearing silently at one's elbow; and at the strangest moment, just when one was convinced that the man could neither hear nor speak, he would for no reason say some memorized piece of English, such as "practice makes perfect," in a tone that turned the proverb dark and mystical.

There were eighteen of us staying in the nursery's little hut suited for six, so on the second night I moved out onto the porch for some oxygen. A gusty night wind was bringing a thunderstorm our way. When one of the farmers awoke and understood that I intended to sleep outside, he began a lament that woke the others who then joined him in making a mighty ruckus. "Doctor Martin, please come in! Please!"

Dhurgastanis are deathly afraid of the spirits they believe stalk about in the dark. Never would one of them sleep outside alone as I wanted to do. But the raw wind was refreshing after the cramped staleness of the hut, and I did not want to go back in. I could not get the farmers to quiet down in their concern for me. Suddenly the night watchman was sitting beside me without coming out of the hut's doorway. He seemed to enjoy the weather as well. The trees were doing a frenzied dance now, leaves raced along the ground, lightning lit the sky behind the hills. "Are you not frightened?" he asked from his treasury of English.

I had not been until that instant, but the thought of spending the night out on the veranda with that fellow was worse than tales of spirits or the howls and pleading of the farmers. I consented to moving back into the stuffy hut, and everyone settled down once more.

The next day we had moved on up the valley and were staying with a kind Tamang family on what passed for a prosperous farm in this area. I was bone weary and could make no conversation with my host, but I was glad of the plate of rice and lentils set on the ground before me and of my sleeping bag to crawl into afterwards.

Who knows what time it was when I woke up suddenly? The room was so dark that I could not tell that my eyes were open. It was another crowded room with bodies paving the entire floor. I could hear the sound of contented sleepers everywhere about me. It took some time for me to realize what had disturbed me—I had evidently been food poisoned, and it was only a matter of time before I was going to be violently sick.

That distant warning signal was distressing enough, but I could not for the life of me recall the layout of the room. *Where was the door; where was my backpack with my flashlight? Stay calm, Martin; mind over matter*, I reminded myself naively. *You're not nauseous.*

When it comes to the digestive tract, I will take matter over mind any day. The warning signals on my dashboard were now all blinking.

Besides sleeping people, your typical pitch black Dhurgastani home is filled with other obstacles to step on: sleeping dogs, sleeping geese, a bucket of buttermilk, the ashes from last evening's fire. I managed to find all of these in the noisiest, messiest manner possible. And the ceiling is not much better than the floor; the beams were designed with someone significantly shorter than a North American in mind. The door, finally found by accident among the snarling, honking, cursing and crashing, was an elaborate system of unpredictable bolts and ingenious locks.

It was a harrowing couple of minutes racing against that emphatic biological clock, and I reached the freedom of outside with no time to spare.

The night was cold; shredded clouds streamed through the moonlight. Much too cold to stay outside for long. During the course of that long night I got well acquainted with the route past the children, dogs and geese. It was not good preparation for another long march in the morning. All that I could force upon my treasonous stomach was oranges.

This American, like a wounded bear when sick, wants only to be left alone to moan in his agony. Some brave soul might come in periodically with an aspirin and to rearrange the pillows, but that is the most from visitors that I can endure. Dhurgastanis, however, have an entirely contrary view to convalescence. The patient is not, under any circumstances, to be left alone for a moment. That would be to communicate a lack of concern. Visitors may completely ignore the patient, cackling around the bed telling stories, but do not leave him to suffer alone.

My well-wishers were a great incentive to force myself up and on the trail. I could not carry my pack so a porter was enlisted to take it on. I overheard a discussion about someone to carry me also, but in an outburst of stupid pride, I promised myself to be portered in a basket only after I dropped dead.

The week's struggles came from without in the elements and the heat, in the narrow, almost imaginary, paths along the eyebrows of a frightful cliff, in my weak language skills and in the disappointed expressions of the farmers when introduced to the new doctor-sahib. Struggles also arose from within: my digestion and embarrassment over my physical weakness. I gave in and got homesick; I got angry with the older missionary who seemed unaffected by all of the hardships. He did not get sick; he did not get tired. Finley appeared to know everyone we saw on the trail and to understand everything that was jabbered at him in the endless farmer meetings that I stumbled to and barely managed to breath through. I got angry with the farmers for expecting me to understand their questions. I got angry with Joanne for spending a comfortable week in

Bhadrapur, looking for a house near our project. And, if the whole truth must be told, I got angry with God for getting me into this place and then deserting me.

The purpose of the week was to gain a first-hand appreciation for the living conditions of the farmers that I was to teach. In retrospect, the time most certainly accomplished that; and God, most certainly, never deserted me. I had asked to meet Dhurgastan, and He had, in spite of me, answered the request.

I returned to the guesthouse in Rajdhani having eaten nothing for five days except oranges. The mission hostess, bless her heart, was serving pizza that evening; and all of the tables in the tiny dining area were set because, besides five missionaries, there were to be thirteen visiting Norwegian hydroelectrical engineers.

The Scandinavians, however, got excited out in the Asian capital and forgot to sign themselves out for dinner. Pizza for eighteen with only five attending.

People still speak of that night in awe. Hushed tones are used of that evening when one American veterinarian ate pizza intended for thirteen engineers. There were no leftovers to face as pizza soup.

I spent the next day recuperating in the garden, reading my accumulated mail. Then I turned to a newspaper that gave the story of how that week at a London auction house Van Gogh's painting of sunflowers was sold for umpteen million dollars. I was staggered; the figure paid was enough to run our entire Mission of four hundred and twenty people for seven years. It was the wrong story to read after my time out among the hardships on the back side of those hills . . . just over there. I could see them from the garden. There is still no church in those barren hills, just that one believing farmer. The paper said the painting's new owner was a secret. That, at least, I could understand. If I had bought a small piece of canvas for such a price when my money could have accomplished so much good, I wouldn't want anyone to know my name either.

People frequently write to remind me of Psalm 46:10, "Be still, and know that I am God." Tremendous, but until yesterday I had never noticed the second half of that verse, "I will be exalted among the nations, I will be exalted in the earth!" Amen and amen. We must be still; He must be exalted. The paradox (of cosmic proportions) that lies sandwiched uncomfortably between those two is that His plan intends on using our struggles and efforts to bring out the promised exaltation.

Your son,
Martin

It takes effort

Do not let yourself get in the way; allow God to work. True advice so far as it carries you. Certainly, apart from God's strength we can accomplish nothing of lasting value. In fact, apart from Him we can accomplish nothing at all because "in Him we live and move and have our being." This is the trumpet call to dependence. This dependence, however, has nothing in common with passivity. Fear of "getting in the way" has been known to keep people from doing God's will as He has clearly presented it to us. "Let go and let God" is not an excuse to pamper ourselves. The Apostle Paul, it must be agreed, burned a lot of calories seeing to the planting of the early Church.

One hears stories in Dhurgastan of people finding portions of a muddy Christian tract along a path somewhere. Three years later when a foreigner moves into the area to do a survey for a drinking water system, the person shows up at his door with the worn remains of the tract asking how he may become a Christian. It just so happens that the foreigner is a missionary and is happy to give an answer.

Such things happen, but it would be a poor mission's strategy to rely upon them. Much more commonly people believe as a result of someone's efforts. God could feed the world without any need of cultivation, the miracles with the loaves and fish make that clear, but His normal *modus operandi* includes a heavy emphasis on farming and human effort.

People want missionaries to live on a different, higher dimension than "regular" families; but the disconcerting truth is that designing an irrigation system or teaching someone to type or castrating a bullock all look surprisingly similar whether done by a missionary or by a "regular" person.

I was surprised by the conditions in Dhurgastan. Surprised but not "caught" by surprise; I had expected things to be different from the familiar. A real shock was to find a recognizable routine to my work-a-day existence. Missionaries still must wash their dishes, even if they have to boil the rinse water before using it.

Pound for pound missionaries do more paperwork than they did while working in their home cultures. While at home considered young and inexperienced, they are in their new project counted as expert professionals and valued consultants, and are thereby channeled into administrative responsibilities. They command a larger staff than they are used to because they find themselves higher up the chain of command. They budget and plan and report; inventory, purchase and ship supplies. In our Mission, prior to beginning something new, everyone's advice had to be sought. And once the something was finished, everything was to be thoroughly documented. Otherwise, after your entire peanut crop molded and you wasted a season in your best field, you would learn that a previous agriculturalist had tried the same scheme fifteen years earlier and had had the same dreadful results.

The problem of politics

"There's no fight like a good church fight," goes a horrible piece of common knowledge, and there is certainly great potential for hurt feelings and sprained sensitivities in a missions situation. It is a small, overworked community, and everyone is under strain even when things are running smoothly. But things are never running smoothly, so that last part remains an untried theory.

A big government bureaucrat wants his child to attend the Mission's boarding school in Bhadrapur. He subtly makes his desire known by bringing a contingent of six burly, armed soldiers with him for his chat with the head-master. His boy is in grade six; entrance tests are given only for children in grades four and eight. The headmaster remains firm, but for as long as the official works in the Bhadrapur office of the Department of Transportation, we find licensing our Toyota Land Cruiser a long, tortuous process.

The farm staff refuses to stay after dark even when needed because everyone in the village is aware that the last night watchman was done in by a ghost. The village mayor insists that the new water system's tap be in front of his house or else he will prevent the installation for the entire community. The American parents are adamant: the tutorial class must teach the children to read by using the phonics method; the British protest that this is archaic. The Community Health Programme seethes beneath its calm exterior because the agriculturalist's advice is ignored by the registered nurse in charge of the operation.

August 2

Now I know how the buffalo meat must feel when Joanne tries to cook it into a chewable form. All is pressure. Annual report due, but the records from last year (before I was resident in the project) are incomplete. How can I report on things which I have not seen? I need to finish that work for the library. I suggested the idea, but never meant to be given charge of it. The language supervisor wants me to read all of those Basha pamphlets on animal health and to decide which might be useful for language school. It is time to do the drug inventory in the clinic and one of the technicians is acting suspicious about his stock cabinet. I have warned him that the next infraction, no matter how small, means curtains for him, even though he has worked on the farm for seventeen years. There has been an outbreak of some type of respiratory disease among local buffalos; they don't run a temperature, but they stop eating. We must be seeing half a dozen like that every day. Yadu missed his English lesson yesterday and showed up unannounced today, but I have left only enough time to prepare for tomorrow's youth group Bible study. I have to do a survey of both First and Second Samuel, and there is a lot of new vocabulary for me to go over between now and then. Cobi Raj is getting behind in his correspondence course on office management because I have not had time to translate it for him. His English is first-rate, but the course material from India is needlessly difficult.

Scientific management, is the application of efficiency methods of business organizations by taking into view this complete round of activities, observing and recording results with the object of fixing upon a "standard best" at each stage; then making the results known as widely as possible so that each may know what is on the record, and so that every worker's skill, experience and observation may be available for his fellow workers and the whole business; and also by adopting the education methods and ideals.

One sentence. How wretched; almost as if designed to be incomprehensible.

August 30

Spent most of this week risking my life in the streets of Bhadrapur on the farm's temperamental motorcycle. Had to go fifteen kilometers outside of town every day to visit the location where my visiting vet student is doing a survey on sheep. The government gave away hundreds of Australian sheep, and I'm afraid that we are in the midst of discovering a tragedy; the majority of them died in the first few weeks from internal parasites. So much for transforming Bhadrapur into the hub of a new wool industry.

Otherwise things are routine for the late monsoon season. Mangos are disappearing from the market. The rains are now less frequent and usually fall at night. Instead, we are inundated with a kind of tiny, white moth. Millions of them appeared one day in our closets and cabinets, orbiting light bulbs and making it impossible to read at night.

I've been asked by someone from a mission hospital down near the border to do a series of drawings on the area's most common poisonous snakes. They are called different names from valley to valley, and rather than arguing over the name, the victim will merely indicate which picture looks like the one that bit him.

At work we are busy as we want to be.

The problem of trivialities

Work, they say, equals force times distance, if I remember my physics correctly; and this makes great sense to a missionary. It means that at twelve thousand miles' distance from your home even a little force expended seems to be a tremendous amount of work.

Whole days, maybe even weeks, went by when nothing significant was accomplished. Thousands of trivialities rose up like bandits in the hills and robbed my slow-moving stagecoach of its energy and creativity. Out of paper clips? It may take most of the afternoon to rectify this emergency. Typing a letter takes all morning because of the stream of interrupting visitors who need to talk about: the fellowship meeting Friday evening, the need to repair the broken plow, why they can no longer work with Tej in milking the goats. Busy every moment and yet it has the texture of practice back in the United States; it feels far removed from "things of eternal value."

The missionary must change what it is that he classifies as work; otherwise, he falls victim to the Magnetic Office Principle. Because one is nervous about dealing with Dhurgastanis in their confusing elements, there is an incessant attraction to stay safely in one's office and to look busy answering mail. A desk and an imposing office door are armor to keep out all of those sticky Asian situations. The bursting filing cabinet and the four level in-and-out trays impress one's superiors, but after a little experience is mixed with a little meditation, a missionary may learn that more real and worthwhile work can be accomplished by sitting in a tea shop all morning. This, however, looks anything but impressive to authorities. But they may be victims of the Magnetic Office Principle themselves.

Once a year the Mission's agriculturalists all pushed away from their desks, then hiked, bussed or flew in from their posts in order to gather together and discuss events. We hoped to share what lessons we were learning that could be applied elsewhere. The day only showed, however, that each of us had fallen for the principle—discussing the advantages of the latest daisy wheel equipped with Basha characters, or arguing the strengths of a new reporting format, defining with great care the difference between goals and guidelines. Everyone had fallen for it except Tokatsu.

This brother did not look impressive; in fact, written communications from Tokatsu were a rare and valuable commodity. When you got a note from him, it was going to be something pithy and necessary. He was a missionary from Japan, and his every expression and mannerism was invested with the elegance of his people. He and his family were posted a six-hour walk over a pass and through a leech-infested hibiscus forest from the hospital in Shujabad.

I had heard a lot of criticism of Tokatsu. But something in the tone of his detractors left me suspecting that much was left unsaid, that the critics felt threatened by someone truly outstanding: he was a loner unable to cooperate with anyone; he had to have his own way and disliked other missionaries; he identified too closely with the surrounding culture; he was not actually a trained agriculturalist, thus making his judgment unreliable; he and his wife rarely made the trip into the hospital and almost never attended church in Shujabad.

I heard a much different story from the Dhurgastanis. Although Tokatsu had not lived in Bhadrapur for several years, several people in our congregation still became nostalgic and teary-eyed when they spoke of him.

My second year in Dhurgastan I finally had the opportunity to make my judgment. My follow-up travels to visit former students took me over the pass and through the hibiscus to Shujabad. Theirs was a more primitive location than any of the missionaries whom I had visited. They were on the second floor, and we could listen all night as the buffalo turned over in the straw below us. The house was, in fact, indistinguishable from those of the neighboring villagers. Inside they had divided the house into three sections using bamboo mats as screens: the back portion was for storage and cooking, the middle section acted as a bedroom and the front part was a tiny space where visitors could sit to drink tea and discuss whatever was on their hearts.

I arrived exhausted from my journey and was disappointed with their house. I had been secretly hoping for some pampering. Though monastically simple, I found that Tokatsu's wife, Musako, was able to transform even an earthy Dhurgastani interior into a haven both beautiful and comfortable. It was luxurious, though completely deprived of luxuries.

That evening after sundown two or three villagers dropped by for a time of prayer because, though Tokatsu had failed to mention it, there were the beginnings of a church in the area. A book of large laminated charts illustrating Bible stories hung from a rafter in the front room where we gathered. Dhurgastanis in that vicinity are learning that Noah and Samson both had oriental features.

In the morning I asked Tokatsu if I might accompany him to work, but he was strangely ill at ease with the idea. It turned out that "going to work" meant visiting a local hut where farmers gathered to eat boiled potatoes and to trade stories about hard times. There were no tractor implements or baseball caps present; but other than that, it was the same scene repeated every morning in every drug store and bank lobby in small-town Texas.

Tokatsu attended and listened to the latest insect damage and frustrations with the weather, the price of urea fertilizer and about Daju's oxen with the broken pastern over in Umbu. After the tea shop, Tokatsu's rounds led him to check up on old man Adhikari's kitchen garden and to see if Poudel had dug the new latrine deep enough this time.

He had no proper office, no stationery for memorandums; but while the rest of us wasted eloquence upon rival strategies in community development, Tokatsu was seeing that it got done. He maximized his time with the Dhurgastanis and shunned Mission meetings. People, of course, misunderstood and felt threatened by him. Tokatsu had withstood the Magnetic Office Principle, but in Shujabad the tree seedlings were beginning to grow everywhere, there was a new water tank down by the school, bamboo check dams in the eroding gullies and a group of new Christians filled with basic questions.

Tokatsu steered an embarrassingly wide course around his other colleagues. He found that they so often brought with them unneeded, cumbersome baggage.

He and I had an enlightening discussion on indigenization; that is, how and when do we replace expatriate personnel with Dhurgastani workers. Everyone repeated the tired maxim that "our job is to work ourselves out of a job"; but again, Tokatsu's example showed that our theories remained learned talk while he was busy implementing them. Actually, the rest of us were not particularly eager to become obsolete.

The problems are prodigious. Embezzling is a great temptation for a Dhurgastani overseeing a large budget, not because of greed alone, but for the very rational idea that if one's own family is in need of food or education, it is more immoral to leave one's family hurting than to steal from foreigners. Dhurgastani staff might not be able to withstand the pressure from unreasonable government requests. What do we do as a Mission when a Hindu rises in seniority to the point that he is made a project director? Women might be mistreated in a Dhurgastani-managed office. Nepotism would become the rule.

Tokatsu recognized all of the potential difficulties. What he did not share with us was any sense of self-interest. I had met a truly meek person.

CHAPTER 7

Anatomy Lessons

The Local Body of Our Lord

"Suffering is an essential element in the Christian religion, as it is in life. After all, the cross itself is the supreme example. If Christ hadn't suffered, do you imagine that anyone would have paid the slightest attention to the religion He founded? Not at all."

Malcolm Muggeridge

Dear Friends,

Let's go to church in Bhadrapur:

We gather Saturday morning at 7:30 on the ground floor of a house near the boarding school's gate. A Hindu family living upstairs rents it to the members of the church board, because in Dhurgastan a Christian church cannot act as a legal entity. Members of this family wander through the services in order to go out back and milk the buffalo. They are the original church mice. Christian meetings have become the backdrop to their daily life, like the quiet music overheard at a sporting goods store. Background noise; pay no attention to it.

Remove your shoes at the door and leave them piled in the heap of identical plastic flip-flops. If someone walks off with yours it does not rank as much of a catastrophe, although you will never find a pair big enough for your feet again. During the monsoon, the sandals are joined by a forest of identical, black, dripping umbrellas. Find yourself a spot on a bamboo mat; men to the left, women to the right, if you don't mind; but so many people will arrive late that by the end of the announcements the genders are no longer segregated.

Late arrivals do pay a high cost, however. They have no chance at the coveted spots around the whitewashed walls but have to tough out the service in the sea of squirming children and nursing mothers. Ragged Bibles and Basha hymnals are passed around; take one if you happen to be literate. The majority cannot read, and listen as the passage is read aloud by one of the university students. Since hymns have to be memorized by frequent repetition, the repertoire must be limited.

For the most part those attending appear to be low caste, and this is not very surprising when one thinks about it. It costs a Brahman too much in prestige to stoop to becoming a Christian; it is too cruel a demotion. My next door neighbor one day confided to me that he would like to attend the village church, but did I have any idea of how much friction it would generate in his family? No, no. It was out of the question. Impossible. He could not afford so high a price.

A Dhurgastani found guilty of changing his religion faces a year in prison with no statute of limitations. This means that although one had converted twelve years previous, should a local adversary suddenly denounce him to the police, they could take action to arrest him at any time at their convenience. The person who brought about the conversion can be sentenced to six years. It is at baptism that the State views the individual as culpable; and there are, therefore, few communing members even though the tiny room is crowded.

Every person in the room is a story to be told. One dark little man with short white hair brings his granddaughter every Saturday. Two years previously the little girl had been very ill, and in seeking her cure he had exhausted all of the local possibilities. In desperation the old man had turned to the Christians. He had heard that sometimes their foreign God appeared to hear their prayers. Distasteful as it was, he presented her to some of the local believers and surprising things followed. The old man remained a Hindu himself, but explains that since Jesus healed her, the granddaughter is to be raised a Christian.

The bearded Canadian P.E. teacher leads the singing with his guitar and is joined by two of the young men who are eager to play. What is lacking in talent is compensated by enthusiasm.

An offering is taken, and the children are dismissed en masse to meet in another house across the road. Everyone is relieved because this creates a little more floor space.

Texts are read, and there is prayer. An exuberant, old Dhurgastani gentleman missing one of his front teeth is responsible for most of the preaching, and today he gives a lively message which leaves the village women rocking back and forth and cackling into their shawls.

The odd sentence gets translated into poor English; but if your Basha is not up to snuff, you are not going to catch much of the service. Toward the end of the morning the room is getting stuffy; one's feet are snoring and the knees complain. That part of your brain responsible for translation is fatigued from the exercise and the concentration in the room is visibly flagging. Precisely when all factors converge to render the situation unbearable, we are through, stretching and talking outside with our friends like absolutely any other congregation after a service, blinking in the bright sunshine.

Your partner,
Martin

The tremendous need

Despite all of the sensational misconceptions harbored about foreign missions, there remains one bedrock reality of which most churches are certain: there continues to be a tremendous need for cross-cultural missions work.

One holds this bedrock view and is compelled by the holding to do something about the need. The house is put on the market, the station wagon is sold and one's partners buy up the rest of the practice down at the clinic. An incapacitating upper-cut is dealt to one's career, and everything dear and familiar is pared away. One arrives in the new culture and it is not long before the nastiest shock of all occurs: one begins to suspect and then to fear and to despair that the bedrock reality was an illusion after all. You're not needed by the struggling church overseas.

How can this be possible? We all know that the world is weak and sinful, that the pressures of population and immorality grow greater by the day, promising to swamp the resources of the evangelicals.

Yes, all of the disgusting stories are true: one hemisphere suffers malnutrition while the other cheats on its Weight Watchers program. But the eager missionary leaps from the airplane; in his luggage are a profession with which to serve and a faith with which to minister. He breaks his nose when in his hurry he runs head-on into the burgeoning nationalism within his profession and an indigenous church leadership. Send your money, but please do not come yourself.

Dhurgastan suffers from a terrible shortage of veterinarians. Much of the country is days away from the nearest trained personnel. Yet the mood in the Ministry of Agriculture is touchy. They want to tackle their own problems or to ignore them if they so decide. But they do not want a stream of enthusiastic foreigners highlighting their own inabilities and offering shiploads of unsolicited advice. Send your money, but don't bother to come with it.

The Church is small, mistreated and inexperienced. One sees it headed for the same tragedies already weathered in Western Europe and North America. Her young prophets chafe impatiently for their turn at the helm and they do not welcome a new generation of missionaries telling them how to reach their culture for Christ. Send your money please; but at this time your presence is not required.

The new missionary is disenchanted by the reception; sensing that he is not needed by the local colleagues or Christians. Were the sacrifices unnecessary after all?

This is a dangerous moment. The missionary is presented with real choices in how to respond. It is not a sure-fire, foregone conclusion that he will choose the right response. It is a precarious moment, one that must be lived through before the fresh, real vision can be born.

April 3

Dear Folks,

Dad asked about the Church in Dhurgastan. I am not

an expert yet, but I do know that it is growing. The leadership is primarily Dhurgastanis who were converted while living abroad in India. Sadly enough, there is infighting, and schisms are not uncommon. Bhind, a city with only one hundred known believers, must sustain the disgrace of four separate congregations; and this in a land thus far free of denominationalism. Problems arise here as they do at home: large, immature personalities driven by selfish ambitions behind a facade of zeal for God. I met one pastor who was very friendly, almost too friendly, making far too much distinction between the foreigners and the Dhurgastanis in our party. Our initial conversation soon found itself revolving around the need of funds for their building program. Who knows? Perhaps he is legitimate, but the conversation came after someone had warned me that a schism had occurred over his misuse of church money.

The Church here is poor in any case, and very suspect in the eyes of the government. Our own pastor in Rajdhani goes before a court this next week to appeal his conviction and six-year sentence for allegedly baptizing new Christians. It is assumed by everyone that the foreigners pay people to change their religion.

Hindus ordinarily do not worship as a congregation; most rites occur early in the morning and only between a priest and an individual supplicant. Due to this lack of a background, the church leadership here tends to do things that feel very western and out of place, as opposed to "merely Christian." It is okay, I suppose, but it seems impoverished somehow. Why in the world adopt western architecture for church buildings instead of something more culturally suitable and familiar? Worst of all, such things give weight to the lie that Christianity is a foreign religion.

Christ may be unknown to some cultures, but He is foreign to none.

Missionaries in our situation actually can play no formal, recognized role in the leadership of the local church. Some find this distressing; but once I saw the reality of things, I felt freed by this state of affairs. My job is to offer my time and efforts to the church people and to let them decide how to utilize me. We support the congregation in those areas where their own resources are thin.

I enjoy Dhurgastani worship for the most part. They are not as restricted and uptight as we were in Austin. Here, our clapping and singing contain more joy and feel less manufactured or structured by the bulletin's order of worship. Of course, they probably have a better sense of how precious is the good news of Jesus than do people raised where its wonders are considered familiar.

Your son,
Martin

Breaking those barriers

Just as the missionaries seem aloof at first, the local believers are not effusive and overjoyed to meet new missionaries. They are shy of their poor English and cannot understand the missionary's even poorer Basha. Like the senior missionaries, the local church has also suffered at the hands of the Frequent Flyer service; they have seen far too many eager young faces come and go to get excited by another one. They have had too many friendships end in an exchange of addresses.

Both sides are, therefore, bashful; and this bashfulness can harden into accepted policy unless heroic efforts are made. After church on Saturday the Dhurgastanis gather into little groups in which to laugh and gossip, while the missionaries form their own circle. After a few moments, the locals go back to their farms or down to Bhindu's tea shop; the missionaries cross the street to a fancier house for coffee and chocolate cookies.

This is normal and natural; all of the laws of language and culture provide for this state of affairs. But it is the job of a missionary to resist exactly this kind of normal, natural situation. The onus is on the missionary, not the local believer, to carve a place for himself in the other group. Everyone is aware of this tension of two congregations under one roof. It is rare indeed that anyone has the courage to mention it. I know I never did.

Not that things actually stand any differently in Texas where any wide place in the road has two congregations of which to boast: one black and one white. Obviously it is not enough to have Him in common.

Missionaries do give up a lot in order to serve overseas. Mexican food, a necessity for the happy maintenance of any Texan abroad, was nonexistent. Our salaries were not half of what our time would have earned in our home countries. In spite of our sacrificial denial, missionaries stand out like ostentatious, diamond-studded stretch limousines in the adopted culture. Lifestyles and possessions rise up as other unavoidable obstacles, and there is a cutting edge to these issues. When the Dhurgastani church needs a new pastor or wants to rent another farm house, or when a promising Christian young person wants to study at the university, do not the Scriptures compel the wealthy believers to treat their wealth as if it belonged in common with the poorer brethren?

Of course. Never should we shirk our responsibility to obey the bond of love within the Church. But, as with everything else on the mission field, there are unforeseen complications lying like crocodiles among the green river grass.

I had heard the term "rice Christian" used for those attracted to the Church because of the financial gain that might be had by pleasing the foreign missionaries. What I had not realized was how very little it took in a country as poor as Dhurgastan to buy this sort of faith.

Not two hours into our village house in Bhadrapur I had met my first hypocrite. Jeewan was a simian-looking fellow, with great muscular arms hanging from his broad shoulders. His prominent brow was accentuated by an unfortunate haircut. This appearance, at first meeting, was endearing; the wild, primeval beast tamed by the power of the gospel. With time, however, and the unfolding of events he became disgusting.

Every addition to the project's personnel had to discover what lay behind those ingratiating manners for himself. We were, after all, missionaries and could not comfortably approach new arrivals to say, "Watch out for Jeewan. He's a monstrous bad penny. Steer clear of him; and whatever you do, don't give him any help." Even if we chose to warn them, the new people would have only considered us cruel and calloused and helped him in any case.

He had an uncanny knack of finding out the latest scoop on everyone; and, more often than not, his first words upon meeting you were some astonishing bits of intimate detail. "So, your older brother drives a delivery truck?"

He borrowed money from all of us, never to pay it back; he counted on us taking the Sermon on the Mount quite seriously and not requiring it of him. But you had to hand it to him, when Jeewan took a job from you, he worked hard.

"Have you heard about the Lewises? They must return to Australia because their littlest girl cannot adjust. And you know that I have always dug their garden for them. What am I gong to do now that they must leave?"

The simian image grew until you could feel him hating you behind the toothy smile.

Our presence in the village acted as poison for Jeewan. He would have made a good, stable Dhurgastani farmer otherwise. But tasting foreign riches—even in the minutest quantities—left him unable to ever be satisfied with his lot. He would no longer be a Dhurgastani and could never be a foreigner. His evolution stopped, and he became a grotesque dead end.

Jeewan attended the church more or less faithfully and knew his Bible stories well. That is, until someone in the congregation made him mad or a missionary paid more attention to another Dhurgastani in his peer group; then he would disappear from the meetings for months on end and one would hear the most awful tales of his behavior.

Hindu friends told me that we were all fools; that it was common knowledge in the village that Jeewan was an informer for the police. Why did we let him treat us so?

As he got older he got angry more frequently, especially with Raju. Jeewan wanted very badly to be the missionaries' pet, wanted it so painfully much that he acted as his own bad advertisement. Raju was his most serious competition; quiet, sincere, easy to like and to look at, Raju gave of himself to help at church. The missionaries all had a crush on him. He made us feel welcome in a hostile country; he made us feel good about ourselves and our efforts. Raju was a success story that we liked to display.

Jeewan may have known the story of Joseph, but this did

not prevent him from playing the part of the ten older brothers. Envy tore at him on the inside and would break out into ugly scenes, fights with bicycle chains after which he would be gone for a month before returning all weepy with repentance. Seventy times seven; the Church forgave and restored her own.

The village's boys once showed a rare spark of initiative and organized themselves into a soccer team. Bamboo goals appeared on the green in front of our house; they even hired an ex-Indian serviceman to act as coach. There were calisthenics and wind sprints, unheard of organization.

Jeewan was not talented, but he played with his whole heart. This was the sort of thing that he could live for; finally something was doing in the village. He looked even more like a great ape as he went down field and mauled the ball. He was enjoying every moment; but as the team got better, it also got cocky. Jeewan's image was just no longer cool enough for the rest of them. I hate to think how he must have smoldered after the coach sacked him.

He came up to practice from the bazaar the next day, bringing with him a gang of tough characters. There was a big fight, knives were pulled, and the village kids never had a chance against real practiced gangsters.

The soccer team was over. The only attempt at healthy organization of the village's teenagers that I ever witnessed ended because Jeewan had his feelings hurt.

He disappeared from church for two months this time, persona non grata with the whole community. Some of us urged that the church had to make some manner of stand; there needed to be formal discipline for Jeewan's sake and so that the Hindus could see that we took this kind of behavior seriously. The pastor, however, urged us to be patient; no one was to be made an example for the benefit of others. People in the congregation suspected the pastor was afraid of what Jeewan's reprisal would be if the church took action.

Behind every trouble maker lie more problems than the obvious ones, and I began to learn something of Jeewan's homelife. And it was abysmal, with the usual alcoholic father who drank away the money and then abused the family in his hopelessness. Jeewan was in need of love, and the missionaries had offered it to him in their open homes. But once inside, lonely little Jeewan had found more than love; he found a good life about which he had never guessed to dream: cassette players and furniture, electricity, running water, spare time . . .

Cynics said that when he finally needed work badly enough he would show up on someone's doorstep. An opening in the maintenance department was posted at the boarding school's gate, and Jeewan washed up on my doorstep.

Well, the story is not over yet, and I pray that it may end happily. Only God knows.

God and hardship

Such stories tie missionaries to the sterns of two ships sailing in different directions. Jesus commands His followers to compassion. The book of Acts pictures the Church as giving, even in a hostile environment; but experience counsels us to great caution. Wealthy missionaries have to rein in their generosity for the good of people's souls and then have to lie in bed at night and worry over how easy it is to say "no" to those in need.

Such stories are depressingly common, but there are joyful adventures as well. There actually are women who in a vision hear that strangers are coming to tell them about the living God and then a team from the Mission arrives surveying the area for a location suitable for a new technical school. There are people who want to become Christians after seeing a film about the life of Jesus while attending a training course. A youth group begins to grow, both in numbers and in grace.

The darkness can seem impenetrable. The police broke into a church service in the little town of Ghasni. "Come outside and worship at the temple of our gods or suffer the consequences!"

And in Dhurgastani prisons the rules run a little differently; the prisoners have to have some way to purchase and cook their own food. I knew an old man who became a Christian while staying at a mission leprosarium. The disease was stopped, though it left him with hardly any fingers or nose. The experience, however, left him an unsuppressible evangelist. He and an old friend in Katihar would joke that perhaps when they were arrested, it could be together. Not long before I left Dhurgastan, the day arrived when the leper was arrested for preaching, and the friends got their wish, being jailed together. It was an act of mercy, as things turned out. A man lacking fingers and without sensitivity enough in his stumpy hands to even turn the pages of his Bible cannot safely cook for himself. The evangelist would have been in even greater discomfort had not his friend been sent along as well to do the rice and lentils.

God allows His people to suffer at the hands of those who fear His truth; there is no escaping this lesson of history behind some ridiculous piece of positive thinking. That God does not call His followers to undergo pain and hardship is a heresy that could only have arisen in the bloated twentieth century West.

The reality of the suffering, however, does nothing to

diminish the reality of His care for His servants. My experience is that those most eligible to complain of the cost of following Jesus are those least likely to do so.

The glare of Dhurgastan's hardships revealed ninety percent of my spirituality to be only American gimmicks. How does one minister to teenagers? Simple. You do lots of activities with them to prove that you are cool, one of the gang: movies (nothing too racy), ice cream, maybe a ski trip. Then kapow! You punch them in their hopes and fears with the gospel. Or, if dealing with someone a little more thoughtful, you run them through a nifty set of Bible studies that are intellectually satisfying. Presto. Conversion to be followed with books one through five on discipleship.

I found myself in Dhurgastan facing a Tuesday night youth group under the light of a single, anemic bulb. There were no movies, even if someone had enough money to burn on a nonessential. There was no contemporary Christian music to listen to, no concerts to attend, no ski lifts or mugs of hot chocolate. No glossy booklets—besides, several in the group were illiterate. What did I have to offer to these young people?

A happier, clean-cut life? Hardly. Success at work and in their family? Nope.

Accept this Jesus at His word, be obedient to Him with your whole heart, and all that I can promise you is His kingdom. But before you get there, some minor details lie ahead. You will be misunderstood by your families and everyone that you know and that matters to you; your government will count you a criminal and may take steps at anytime to rehabilitate you. It will be hard to arrange your marriage; employers may discriminate against you.

There are not many teenagers in America that I know who would accept such a "good deal."

Prem, Raju and Jalak came by my house after dark. The electricity was off, so we sat around my table in the conspiratorial glow of a single candle. They had come by to pray for me before my departure from the village. I was going back to safety and comfort; none of them possessed a little green passport with gold lettering on it like mine. They would be staying in Dhurgastan, staying in the village, although recently the police had begun to give the church some trouble in earnest. They were neither glib nor anxious. I realized that the often-quoted missionary farewell speech was true in my case: I had indeed gained more from them than they from me.

CHAPTER 8

The Idol Rich

Life with Hindu Neighbors

"Who in the highest heavens guards and watches;
He knows indeed, but then, perhaps He knows not!"
                                        The Rig Veda

Before Joanne and I left for Dhurgastan we spent an evening with a family recently returned from being missionaries there. They were living way out in the country, out in the scrubby hills and down a dark country road that left me certain we were lost just as we arrived. I remember little of the evening except that we were introduced to exotic Asian food soon to be our everyday fare and that after dinner between the four of us we killed seven scorpions who crept in out of the chilly night to see the slide show. Being missionaries, our new friends felt uncomfortable in conversation if deprived of the security of holding the remote control of a slide projector. Toward the end of the evening the man turned to me and said, "Do not expect to get into any theological discussions while in Dhurgastan."

I now understand what he had meant. He was trying to say that most Dhurgastanis give their religion very little critical thought, that the most common reason for performing a given ritual is because their grandfather thought it a good idea and had done it. But at that time I was an impatient tiger, eager for the hunt and thought, "Speak for yourself, buddy. Maybe you couldn't get into those kinds of conversations, but I'm certainly going to. That is the very reason for which I'm going."

Lots of Christians perhaps would not want to get into a theological discussion; that word "theology" is unattractive to them, and they are convinced that in the thesaurus it is followed by synonyms such as: dead wood, needlessly foggy, counterproductive to the gospel. These are the same brethren who remind us earnestly, "Keep preaching Jesus to them, and don't let anything sidetrack you into trivialities." And they are right, in so far as they go; "theology" most definitely can mean all of those useless things, and emphatically Jesus Christ is to remain our Issue of issues as well as King of kings. Nevertheless, Jesus preached to a Hindu with no background or foundation has very little chance and will be sucked into the amorphous blob. He will be taken in hospitably by the Hindu and then put gently on the hearth, the place of honor, along with all of the other petty, household gods to collect dust. No, there is spade work necessary before the soil is ready for sowing.

Trying to shovel mist

Hinduism is not a simple creed nor a definite religion with clear-cut doctrines. As one Jesuit scholar in Rajdhani said to me, "Studying Hinduism is like trying to shovel mist." It is a way of life and a way of thinking as much as a religion, and very nearly defies definition. To prove this, muddle through the first chapters of any book on the subject. You put the book down in disgust, "What is this guy trying to say? Out with it; what do Hindus believe?"

Well, a Hindu can be a polytheist, a monotheist, even an

atheist. What ground lies in common between these? Worst of all, an individual Hindu may wear any of these hats, changing to whichever one is most appropriate for the present situation. A person whose thinking and worship take place within this sort of framework cannot hear your message about Jesus.

Western books on the subject frequently mention the humbling fact that there are allegedly 330,000,000 Hindu deities, obviously a figure able to discourage the most pious in their pursuit of enlightenment. This enormous pantheon acts rather like a huge apartment complex; being so crowded robs an occupant of the desire to meet even the next door neighbor on an intimate level. Just business; nod to one another in the parking lot, but there is absolutely no possibility of becoming fond of each other.

That is perhaps an unfair caricature, however, because some branches of this religion have a strong monism; that is, they consider everything that is to be a part of God. This thought has its appeal, until its final conclusions are plumbed thoroughly. Truth and untruth, existence and nonexistence are all within God; and these are, therefore, in the final analysis all the same thing. Logic is thrown out with the laundry water, and everything loses its significance for the odd reason that all things are considered equally significant and insignificant.

The most prestigious school in all of tiny Dhurgastan is English Medium which overlooks smoky Rajdhani from the rim of the city's valley. The children of all of the most powerful and influential attend. At the school, next to the headmaster's office, where in America would be found words by Thomas Jefferson or Abraham Lincoln, there is a plaque. I found its words symbolic of this whole subject:

> English is the Medium,
> The Medium is the Message.
> The Message is: Nothing is as it
> seems; neither is it any Different.

Not really a thought well suited to encourage teenagers to take their studies seriously. It is a Buddhist thought actually; but in Dhurgastan, religion finds a humid atmosphere, and it grows like creepers do in the jungle. They are intertwined and cannot be separated without doing them damage. This plaque at first reading sounds terribly heavy and spiritual, but careful examination shows it to be only shining swamp gas that chokes any clear thinking.

An average village farmer, of course, is working much too hard making ends meet to give any consideration to the final conclusions of his monism. In any case, they only trundle out that position when some foreigner insists upon everyone getting philosophical. The real meat and potatoes of village life is an unabashed henotheism. This means that, confronted as they are with such a gigantic collection of gods, they act pragmatically by choosing one deity and elevating it to the primary position as the supreme in their devotion.

Indra, our storekeeper at the farm, was a henotheist of the first order. He had decided, for reasons known only to himself, that one of Vishnu's avatars (or incarnations), Ram, was to be his personal god and benefactor.

We discussed the situation as we walked back from a call together. An oxen had fallen and broken a hind leg. Taking a history from the owner I discovered that this was his third animal to break a leg by crashing down precisely the same hill. I told the farmer that we could splint the oxen's leg with bamboo but that in this case prevention was better than cure. Instead of a bamboo splint, what he really required was a bamboo fence around that hill.

In any case, Indra and I walked through the rice fields with the sun beating down upon us, pulling little leeches out of our socks and discussing henotheism. Yes, he supposed that if one got picky that there probably were in fact gods more exalted than Ram; he was, after all, only one of several incarnations of the many gods.

Can you see what response telling Indra about Jesus Christ is bound to elicit? It is the same bone-chilling idea that one begins to hear bandied lightly about in tanning salons and shopping malls in the West: "That's fine for you. That is your path, and I am happy for you that you have found peace in it."

Nice and polite, inoffensive and mushy as a favorite pillow; anything but reasonable.

I did speak with Indra and he responded in approximately that tone, as did my office landlord. He was a really impressive gentleman and the best farmer in our village. Unlike his neighbors, he was always working; and when the fields did not require labor, he was repairing things or out doing some project for the community's well-being. He was a dapper dresser when he was making his rounds and, rather out of character, put henna in his hair to stay vital and youthful-looking. We would often walk along the road together, and he took obvious joy in being able to teach me. Never did he pass me without pausing to explain a new phrase, or to tell me what the day's celebration meant.

Who knows why, but although he disliked many of the missionaries who taught in the boarding school in Bhadrapur, for some reason he liked me and treated me as his slow-witted, but well-meaning son.

He would point to the circles of men sitting under the

trees drinking and playing cards and tell me that it was these useless customs that accounted for Dhurgastan's poverty. In reality those vices do not explain all of the country's ills, but in our village the charge did have something of a ring of truth about it. When I was called out after dark, almost anyone in the muddy streets was going to be incoherent and abusively drunk; sober people did not venture out after sunset.

He was in every way the progressive man, with linoleum on the floor of his house that he swept himself every morning and the cleanest toilet in the village, including those of the missionaries. His wife did not live with him, but owned a small tea shop just down the road and stayed there. It was a very unusual situation, and I could never get to the bottom of it except to learn that they were pained by the sight of one another, which would have to have been frequently, living within earshot as they did.

He asked me one day to come down from my stifling office for tea, and I was happy at the offer. I was only sweating away and falling asleep over some journal articles. I had watched him live out his daily life below me over the course of months, but I had never been in his rooms before. Other than the linoleum, they were routine Dhurgastani interior decorating. In the corner of his room, up high on a narrow shelf, were three or four framed pictures of his favorite gods. These gaudy pictures in brilliant colors are printed by the zillions down in Bombay. Shiva, the Destroyer, smirked down at me, easily recognizable carrying his trident, with a cobra snoozing cuddly around his neck and the white bull lounging at his feet. Another picture was of his elephant-headed son, Ganesh, the patron of all auspicious beginnings. With the portraits were the charred remains of that morning's incense, and dabbed about the walls were little globs of straw and cow manure. Hinduism is graphic and colorful, unashamed to assert itself as a spectacle to any of the senses. Missionary Protestantism can look as drab as an accountant's wardrobe in comparison.

His daughter-in-law brought us our tea and returned, leaving us to smile at one another. He followed my gaze to the pictures and began what he considered my religious education. His vocabulary got the best of me when he began telling tales of Krishna's exploits with the young shepherd girls.

He acted the perfect host and paused in my catechism to make it clear that he had only the greatest respect for the God that I had followed to Dhurgastan. In fact, from what he could tell, the Christian's God was better able to motivate His followers into doing deeds of kindness and devotion.

I pondered the state of religion in America and then assured him that we had our own share of marginal disciples.

This respect for my foreign God brought him to the usual punch line: we, of course, as thinking men of the world realized that were we only to go back far enough through the curtains backstage, we would find that all distinctions would be swallowed up into the ineffable void that lies even beyond personality.

He smiled, and well could he afford to; after all, this made us brothers. The fact of our brotherhood was obscured only by the illusions created by men's silly doctrines. His gods and mine were really only smaller pictures of the real One. Any god that can be expressed in word or comprehended in thought is not the real One.

Here was religion at its most tolerant, willing even to sacrifice itself in the search for harmony in all things. How could I possibly be so ill-mannered and dogmatic as to disagree with his fine example?

It is at this point where Jesus requires His followers to be impolite and to unsheathe that sword which He said that He came to bring to earth.

We went out onto the sunny veranda and looked over the millet growing in his fields. I attempted to disagree with a framework that prides itself on being able to assimilate even its enemies. I tried to show him that he actually did not live within that framework and, in reality, did not believe the words that he had said. This raised an eyebrow; what he had said was pretty standard Dhurgastani orthodoxy.

"Older brother," I said. "If we asked two men who was the real prime minister, they might give us different answers." I stepped to my right and jerked a thumb knowingly to my breast. "It is Bim Bahadur," I exclaimed, supremely confident. Then I moved to my left, "No, no. I know the minister personally. He is my friend, Mohan Adhikari." I stepped in between the two imaginary answers and looked at my landlord who was following the display with more than an academic interest. "You see, older Brother, this is a silly example; we know that Mr. Bahadur or Mr. Adhikari might be the real prime minister. But we also know that they cannot both hold the office. The man on the right could be correct . . . or the man on the left . . . or they could both be mistaken. But they cannot both be right in their thinking; the things each said cannot both be true."

The law of noncontradiction is basic to all clear thinking. If the sum of the two numbers is six, it cannot also be seven. Surprisingly enough, discussing that law can also be basic to explaining Christianity in Dhurgastan, and Americans more and more have to be reviewed in it like old algebra lessons. (I knew it at one time; but that was, oh . . . years ago.)

Merely different languages

Talk about Jesus to a Hindu and he will tell you how all religions are merely different languages for the same concept. Tell an American about your work in missions and he will bellow in reply, "Who are you to be foisting your foreign religion on those poor, uneducated people?" Actually, the Hindu and the American are saying the same thing: they both assume that all religions, even seriously conflicting ones, are equally true and that there is no question as to finding out which one is the real background tapestry of the whole universe.

One may disagree with Islam, but it at least retains unshifting ground upon which to joust about truth. Not so in Hinduism, Buddhism and Taoism. These view logic as a constriction, a limiting restriction which must be risen above in order to arrive at the dimension of pure spirit. Christianity, however, describes logic not as a low, primitive rung on a cosmic ladder, but instead as a circle drawn in dark paint. Outside of this circle is not spirit, but irrationality.

My landlord got the point: what was obvious about prime ministers was more than likely accurate for God as well. The idea intrigued him. Seed was sown.

Conversations such as that one usually did not take place in English but were in Basha; therefore, I was at a stiff disadvantage in an argument. But things would have been positively wonderful had that been the only complicating factor that I faced as a messenger. Sadly it was not; a more ugly disadvantage was that in reality I am a frightened, hesitant evangelist. Such a discussion's approach has on me much the same effect as Joanne's "Oh honey, your dentist appointment is for this afternoon, remember?" The pulse receives the message and responds; the mouth goes dry and the tongue thickens until it resembles an old knee sock. An obnoxious mental buzzer goes off like when you are about to lock the keys in the Volvo.

If this is one's reaction to vacuum cleaner salesmen or door-to-door evangelism in the home culture, then beggars and witnessing to the gospel overseas are going to produce a similar disquiet. Everyone concedes the point; nothing is magically transforming about becoming a missionary; but conceded or not, we still harbor the secret dream that "if the scene was changed I would be bold as a lion. If I could only get overseas, oh what great things I might do."

Western peoples, and in my experience especially Americans, are uptight and defensive as hermit crabs about religion in general. In an encounter on the topic both the proselytizer and the proselyte-to-be are incapacitated by their anxiety. They may hide behind false bravado and feigned confidence, but in such an atmosphere of fear, clothed in fake assurance, there is almost no chance that real communication will survive. The conversation is stillborn even if the contestants persist in keeping up appearances for a long time. The Christian was out to convert, not to listen; and the non-Christian calls up the reserves to repel the attack and does not listen.

"No one's gonna do any converting around here, Mack. What's the matter, can't you read? No solicitors."

Thankfully, Dhurgastanis are not burdened with a set of whistles and sirens quite as hair-triggered as that. They cannot afford to be because caste rules, marriage customs, their career and daily habits, even the calendar filled with festivals . . . everything in that society is richly marinated in Buddha-Hinduism. If he were uncomfortable with religion, a Dhurgastani's life would be one constant excruciating migraine. My pulse would pound like I had been running the bleachers at basketball practice, but they remained calm: why shouldn't they?

My next door neighbor confided to a Peace Corps veterinarian who stayed for a while with us that he had lived next door to Christian missionaries for twelve years watching their odd behavior. During that time, he said, none of them had ever come over to his house for the express purpose of explaining to him "the good news" (his words). He can be forgiven for entertaining the obvious thought that if it were such good news the foreign visitors would want to tell him about it. He did not understand our twelve-year paralysis. The only Dhurgastanis that I found to be frightened by religion were those that had picked it up, along with communism, in their higher education at university.

Good, meaty "theological" discussions are out there for the taking, if one is serious about creating opportunities. He might be sitting in a tea shop, its interior and occupants blackened by the smoke within its tiny walls. A funeral procession happens by on its way down to the river where the deceased is to be cremated. First come three or four fellows carrying great curved metal horns the size and shape of elephant tusks. They pause every thirty feet and produce a mournful blast, the kind of noise that might be made by the elephant bereft of its tusks. Next comes the body, wound tightly in cloth or plastic, carried by several relatives; and finally come the rest of the mourners in a long string, each with a piece of firewood hefted on his shoulder.

My friend Steve would turn to the other customers in the tea shop and ask what they supposed happens to a person after his death. In America this would be particularly bad form to ask at a drugstore counter after watching a hearse go by behind two motorcycle cops; but in Asia it seemed perfectly natural. Everyone was already thinking about it. A theological discussion was bound to follow.

Not everyone in the Mission admired Steve for his honesty. Many of the brethren insisted that their work, forty hours minimum of assigned labor, was their profession of faith and sufficient for most occasions.

Surely this is the old, unnecessary argument without any tread left on it. Does anyone seriously contend that there exists a real, unavoidable conflict between the interests of work and word? Without a doubt the two must speak with one voice or else it sounds like my shortwave radio drifting back and forth between Radio Moscow and Voice of America. We have all known and tried to avoid the bold, would-be evangelist who lost all credibility because of the sorry job that he did at his desk or the tyrannical way that he oppressed his secretary. On the other hand, what we cannot say is how many of those nice, responsible, competent people that we have worked with are closet disciples of Jesus.

In Dhurgastan I was a stranger, a foreigner, and everything that I did lived up to that description: very strange and very foreign. If I was punctual and industrious, never misplaced a penny or lost my temper (sadly, none of these were consistently true of my performance); all of these inexplicable things and virtuous characteristics would be lost among all of the other inexplicable things that I did every day. People appreciate foresters or veterinarians or tunnel engineers who do an excellent job at their tasks, but not one can translate that appreciation into knowledge of Christ crucified and resurrected.

But in a land where evangelism with the intention of persuasion is against the law, is not our work the only voice allowed us?

I was often asked why we went to a country that restrained our Christian voice instead of going somewhere open to the preaching of the gospel. There are several answers to that question; and yes, those laws did hinder our efforts to render the love of God understandable to our neighbors. But actually, I can understand why those laws were enacted and even, after a strange fashion, thank God for them. Violent India battles with itself to remain a single secular state. The British partition of the subcontinent left Moslems and Hindus sitting in each other's laps, and, in consequence, tensions erupted into horrible communal feuds. The torch that finally sets fire to the powder often seems impossibly insignificant to a Western mind. And Dhurgastan's situation is similar, with its many different peoples and their varied ways. Can Hindus sit idly by and watch the Mohammedans slaughter holy cows? Can a Moslem tolerate idols being carried past his house in a procession?

They have to step lightly. One spark from a heel and kaboom! Villagers who have known each other from childhood can be slitting one another's throats.

This does not, however, justify those laws. Too many people in power merely use them to protect the Hinduism which enshrines the status quo. They recognize in Christianity the great equalizer to caste, race and wealth. Those laws, which are unjust and do violence against man's freedom to follow his conscience, do prevent most open air evangelism and wholesale distribution of tracts and Christian literature; but I have always considered those the least successful techniques in any case. No laws yet prevent neighbors from sharing their beliefs out on a sunny veranda or while sharing a crowded taxicab.

Governments around the world are getting more cagey in

their attempts to gag missionaries. This is the undeniable trend. Lines are being drawn more and more exactly in order to preclude real evangelism while still allowing for the inflow of aid money. When those lines constrict into an unavoidable situation, missionaries are faced with few, unhappy alternatives: everyone packs up and goes home, leaving the indigenous Church in God's hands; change the organization into a humanitarian outfit, dropping all pretense at being Christian at the project level or they may go to jail. They do not have the option of not speaking of Him who sent them.

When trends and events make us anxious, we should remind one another that these are nothing new at all.

CHAPTER 9
_____

Working between Missionaries

"Materiam superabat opus."*

Matthew Henry

Dear Friends,
High Adventure: Katihar, east of Rajdhani, is one of the
Mission's more remote projects. Tucked under the chin
of a rocky hill there is a twenty bed hospital serving an
area population of four hundred thousand. There are
also literacy classes running every night of the week;
and, of course, there is agricultural work that includes
the animal health trainees that we teach in Bhadrapur.
Part of my job is to visit these farmers and insure that
they are putting into practice what they have learned.

So Joanne and I found ourselves wheeling dizzily over
terrain so convoluted that it would send a mapmaker
back to college in search of a new career. The flight was
canceled yesterday because of rain, and today we buzz
the strip once in order for the pilots to get a good look
at the red clay surface. Take your time, fellows, because
if it is still too slick, the small landing area ends in a
rickety fence that is meant to warn you that you are
about to topple over the lip of a gorge which is impressive even by Dhurgastani standards.

The work exceeds the material.

Of course we landed safely (I'm writing you our monthly prayer letter, aren't I?), but I must admit that the rickety fence was closer to the nose of the plane than I appreciated.

I have spent the past three weeks tramping my legs off around these hills, meeting with the farmers and making plans for future work in the area. It has been a great adventure visiting among the different tribal peoples: Rais, Muggers, Gurungs, even the famous Sherpas. Each people has its own maze of customs to be navigated: a Rai must sacrifice a pig and have plenty of alcohol on hand in order to perform his religious rites; a Brahman, perish the thought, is never to touch either a pig or alcohol; and to the Chhetries, it matters what kind of a pig that you are talking about.

As great a privilege and adventure as life among the tribals was the opportunity of getting to know my missionary colleagues in the project: Dr. Phebe Uy from the Philippines; Bob, a heart surgeon from San Diego, spending three months away from his busy practice, doing the minor surgeries that have accumulated since the last volunteer surgeon's visit; and the best missionaries that I've watched in action, Setoshi and Musako Tokatsu from Japan, working in a village even more remote than the hospital.

What can I say? What have I done to deserve to wander through all of this beautiful country, to serve these good people, to make friends of such marvelous saints? Absolutely nothing; I feel like an imposter. What little Joanne and I may have given up in order to come here has certainly been repaid us in a better currency; but that's one of the benefits that Jesus promised to His servants.

High Sacrifice: Sometimes my visits would take me away from Joanne and the hospital for several nights, off to exotic places like Umbu, Maryastan and Shujabad; other times I could come back to the hospital with its coughing generator and electricity (six to ten p.m.). On those days, leaving early in the noisy Dhurgastani morning or returning home under an afternoon's crashing thunderstorm, I always paused at a certain place on the rocky steps leading down to the hospital. There rest two, quiet, raised rectangles of piled stones. One is large, the other small. Graves are rare in a Hindu country and so I asked what stories they told.

Under the larger sleeps an old leader in the Dhurgastani church, a worker at the hospital for seventeen years. The smaller is the three-year-old daughter of some German missionaries. She died unexpectedly of dysentery before any of the doctors took her condition seriously; and in their sadness the family went home. They later returned to Dhurgastan, and I realized with a twinge that it was that joyous couple just down the path from where we were sleeping in the guesthouse.

I like to stop at those graves and catch my breath. It brings a sweet nostalgia and a quiet pride that I hope is of the godly variety. To serve the Lord God has always cost the servant in terms of years, in terms of families, in terms of lives. We forget that as we scramble for self-fulfillment and chase our petty ambitions; but sacrifice has always been the rule, though we prefer to consider it the exception.

May God be pleased with us all, and do with us as best honors Him.

Your partner,
Martin

The problem with relationships

Is a chapter on "relationships between missionaries" really called for? Isn't it a little self-indulgent? After all, it is not for other missionaries' sakes that one goes overseas.

True enough; most assuredly one does not become a foreign missionary in order to stew in an ecumenical fellowship. Yet, I believe it was Bill Gothard who first shocked me with the cold steel of the situation: most missionaries return worn out and disgusted not because of yellow fever or Islamic fundamentalist terrorism but because of deep, raw frictions with other missionaries.

I know; I was incredulous when I heard it, too. If these ambassadors of the gospel are unable to subjugate little, personal tensions for the sake of breaking into a dark society, then what hope is there?

Very little apart from God's grace, apparently.

Before we get too high and mighty, however; let's be brutally honest with ourselves. We have all worked on church boards or committees or some other behind-the-scenes body; and we know that on those small councils fierce rivalries form between insufferable personalities. Schemes and intrigues go on that would make the most corrupt of Popes blush. Now imagine that those same insufferable people live near you and that you are called to work and worship with them on an almost constant basis. They are, in fact, the only English speakers with whom you can readily communicate within three-days' walk. You get to know each other's tiniest mannerisms and idiosyncracies: just how strong they like their coffee, who they dated in high school, those same stupid jokes over and over again. What would be no more than a small irritating squeak in the home culture, turns into a major malfunction under the boiling, sweatshop conditions of your remote project. The manifold cracks, pistons seize, the radiator hose bursts, steam goes everywhere and everyone gets burned.

Some say that all of this happens because missionaries depend too much upon one another instead of bonding to their new culture. These people restrict new missionaries to a single piece of luggage and refuse to meet them at the airport; those first days of "bonding" are to be done alone, just you and the culture. Hotels are off limits; one must find a place to stay that first night with a local family by asking passing strangers if they know of a room available. Only after the passage of significant time is contact with the Mission allowed. The goal of this torture is that the new arrival will learn to need the local surroundings and can do without the unhealthy congestion of a safe, foreign subculture.

In veterinary college I once had a baby goat bond to me, and I barely survived the experience. Its mother had not survived the delivery, and the kid required bottle feeding every three hours. Its first night was filled with my face, waking it up and giving it sustenance; so a little confusion on its part is excusable. The rascal would follow me around, and if prevented from going with me into a lecture, would bleat and kick up an amazing ruckus. I, therefore, understand the concept.

A new missionary must learn to face, and even to initiate, uncomfortable, unfamiliar situations; otherwise he can rapidly be isolated and insulated from the very society which he came to serve. Immersion in the culture is a good thing. Nevertheless, caution must be exercised because immersion can be the step just previous to drowning in the culture. We can each tread water for different lengths of time.

Our own Mission went in for this bonding idea with a hearty vengeance which it later had to modify. The program created a stupefying impression of sheer terror in some people who later went on to prove themselves capable at cross-cultural survival. Some who would have done fine if allowed to slowly test the waters instead were drowned because of our insistence on doing it right. Room must be made for different personalities: there are those who enter an unheated swimming pool with one mad abandoned dash; others go toe by cautious toe.

Joanne and I bonded, I suppose, with our Language and Orientation Class. The first person to meet me at the guesthouse that disorienting night was Gerard Liston-Pym in his bow tie and flashy silk blazer with its sleeves rolled up to the elbows. He explained to us in an effusive Oxbridge accent that such sleeves were trendy in London just then.

If the senior missionaries made the first impression of a side of refrigerated beef, then Gerard Liston-Pym brought images of the ladies bridge club, and I was left to piece it all together.

Our group dribbled in off of international flights for the next two days; and the final, assembled, fully articulated organism was strange and wonderful indeed. Twenty-one adults (plus numerous children) from eight countries and four continents. We were nurses, accountants, physicians, a forester, a maintenance man, two housewives and a veterinarian. Our English suffered from every insulting accent, and it was a sweet sound to hear us together—like feeding time at the parrot house.

We were Anglicans of the high and low persuasion, Mennonites from the farmlands where they settled after the European persecutions, Presbyterians from splintered denominations not on speaking terms back home, Calvinists from the Reformed Reformed Church (no kidding), Lutherans and Free Church ("free" from state-imposed Lutheranism). A couple of us went to great lengths to avoid any religious filing system that the others could devise. We had baptized our babies and forbidden it, served both the cup and the bread to the laity, or the bread alone. Zealous adult converts and people who could not remember disbelieving.

Conversations were intense, and anything under the sun was fair game and in season. There was a South African brother with a face that seemed to be constantly squinting off across a vast plain; an Irishman who spoke about the plight of Bangladeshis in Belfast. I found myself ardently defending policies of the United States which I had voted against.

We were all Christians, but there was precious little common subculture with which to safely bond.

January 28

After dinner a group of us relaxed upstairs and had an interesting experience playing the old game Password. We had divided ourselves into teams that left Brits giving clues to Americans and some funny miscommunications resulted. (A Welshman in the no-uncertain-terms tone of that race informed us that "Taffy" had absolutely no philological connection with "Saltwater.") Beneath the silly laughter lies perhaps a lesson for Christ's Church to ponder.

Christian community—that is disciples living in close proximity in order to better work and worship together—is a romantic situation for only the first three days, if that long. Then comes the demanding work. Courage and vigilance are necessary in order to keep short accounts with one another. Only those who have never tried life in such circumstances can envision it as a constant, peaceful coexistence accompanied by Gregorian chants in the background.

February 21

Fellowship time at Prem Sadan guesthouse last night. My thoughts have been wicked and judgmental: "Oh, you can tell she's liberal (theologically or politically, it makes no difference)," or "He's not going to make it. You can see that he is not right for a place like Dhurgastan." Petty jealousies, envy at their better language ability, anger over how they always slam their door too loudly, their pesky, whining three-year-old. . . . How does one fight this sort of thing? Thought control cannot mean not having an emotion occur; I can't stop them. Prayer for someone on my nerves is harder than memorizing the day's vocabulary, and that is a real grind.

Our experience was extremely "ecumenical," a word that conjures up deadly thoughts in an orthodox mind like mine; but then, orthodox by whose standard? The Scripture's, of course; but then, by whose interpretation?

It helped to drop the labels and deal instead with personalities. A certain denomination now no longer exists for me. When it is mentioned I see Cleve's face and his impish grin. I could distrust some distant group of dubious reputation, but I must love Cleve—the brother with the tender heart and the sense of humor that thrived on practical jokes. Who would have thought that with our severe baggage restrictions someone would have brought a wig and masks to Dhurgastan? When did a physician as talented as he find time to learn how to juggle?

There is both good and bad in the ecumenical experience; but we found the good to swamp the bad, and the time for us was very blessed.

The next time you are on a plane to Las Vegas, turn to the passenger next to you and introduce yourself as a missionary. If the conversation by some miracle does not die instantly upon impact, then it will not be long before it turns compass-like to "the hypocrites in the Church" and "the evil of denominationalism." Even passengers never claiming to be Christians, and perhaps especially those people, have a strong sense that "if Christianity were true, then it should be lived to the hilt. All of those who purport to be following Jesus should do so in love and unity." Everyone agrees with the gist of this sentiment, but the wars of history and the schisms of the centuries prove how difficult it is to do in practice. Tolerance as a concept is manifestly popular; as an actuality it is an endangered species not even present in the fossil record.

Relationships between missionaries are really stories of unity being forged in an oven heated by every problem that the office and religion, personality and raunchy environment can shovel in.

We found ourselves in Dhurgastan eating bad food and drinking boiled water with people we would have previously been happy to pronounce apostate; but after some conversation, we often found a fellow servant of the same Master, pulling as one with us in the great cause.

The problem with stereotypes

Americans, if we believe the stereotype, are for the most part New World idealists who believe that all things are possible and that yes, their daughter could become president if she works hard enough and applies herself. Scandinavians find us rather silly and exhausting if taken in large doses. On the other hand, they are not as quick to speak their mind and do not wear their intimate thoughts on the outside of their parkas for them to get frostbitten. The difference is a very real one and affects the two groups dramatically when they attempt to live together.

Of course there are extroverted Norwegians and cautious Americans, but the terrifying thing about stereotypes is not that we unfairly use them, but that they are so frequently correct. It insults our sense of democracy.

Our Americans were of the sunny, idiotic variety; and they believed in fervent, vocal corporate prayer. The very idea of praying aloud and apart from the moorings of liturgy was distasteful to the quiet religion of the Norwegians. In consequence, the Americans considered the Norwegians stuffy and unspiritual (and of course said so); while the Norwegians thought the Americans shallow, presumptuous and unspiritual (and would not say it). By definition merely "talking out" our differences is part of the problem, not the simple solution to being together, because we even handle our differences differently.

There are, as stern brothers remind us, dangers to ecumenicalism. There is a slippery slope down which to slide into oblivion, the other side of the horse from which to fall. Tolerance, when not critical, can decay into syncretism. This is the great mistake of Hinduism and of the vague new spiritualities making the rounds of the West, taking the pleasant from every source and stabbing truth a mortal blow in the sweet name of understanding. We forget, then remind ourselves, then forget again that sincerity proves very little, that people are frequently sincerely wrong.

We say this and yet with the next breath have to admit that we cannot claim to hold the correct opinion or statement of faith. If my statement or creed that aims to incorporate the simple "nonnegotiables of the faith" has ten points, immediately I have divided Christendom into at least three groups: my group, those who feel there is an eleventh point of such importance that it must be added, and those who feel that the first nine were quite sufficient—that tenth one being a picky bit of trivia.

So we may all despair of ever grasping properly even the basics on this side of the grave, but just because the night is foggy does not mean that we are justified in abandoning the wheel to the current. A missionary who loses all conviction as to absolute truth is untethered and drifts ineffectually. The ugly fact is that Jesus was obnoxiously insistent (to our sensitive ears) upon His unique relationship with God.

We all must plant our flag and defend that idea until the ammunition is exhausted and we fall to a man. But it leaves plenty of issues over which to forget the common foe and to draw sabers against each other. Doctrinal issues such as the virgin birth, the baptism of the Holy Spirit, the inerrancy of the Scriptures, the events surrounding the Lord's return. And issues of behavior: smoking, drinking alcohol, attending Hindi movies down in the bazaar, discipline of children.

Some of my most harrowing times in Dhurgastan were when I was asked to lead a project Bible study meeting. Unless I restricted myself to pabulum, people to either side of me on the ecclesiastical spectrum were going to be offended by my words.

I have dwelt on the negative touchy aspects of missionary relationships because no one needs to be forewarned of good times. (Watch out! Be careful! You're in for a wonderful time.) Our experience was not uniformly rosy, and yet it was fertile and thrilling. The long evenings by candlelight because the electricity had failed again, deprived of television and all those distractions of back home that really render us poorer. Sipping hot coffee and sharing with each other of our struggles and victories. Long tales of interesting childhoods in far off lands. Testimonies of how one's God works similarly in the lives of people on different continents. It is a taste of how very ebullient and varied the kingdom of God shall be in its final consummation.

CHAPTER 10

The Industry

Some Changes in Missions

"Never allow the thought—'I am of no use where I am'; because you certainly can be of no use where you are not."

Oswald Chambers

The term "veterinary missionary" conjures in people's minds an image like a photograph I once saw. It was taken in West Virginia or backwoods Tennessee and was no joke. They had lined up a farmer's horses, a sleepy mule, a dairy cow and a pig or two and there was a zealous young fellow preaching to them, walloping a big black Bible of the size that most of us inherit from a grandmother—the kind that instead of being put on the coffee table could itself do service as a piece of furniture. The fellow no doubt had a sermon of three points (each point alliterative and beginning with the letter "p") and was doing an exuberant job of exegesis. Study of the photograph revealed his audience's attention to be about as lively as that of any other congregation.

Ah, the clergy have an uphill struggle!

If while filling out the paper work for a Dhurgastani resident's visa one were to enter "missionary" or "church-planter" in the space labelled "occupation," one would receive about the same welcome were one to write "violent Islamic fundamentalist" in the same blank on a U.S. application. No thank you. Rejected for unspecified reasons. Sure thing, buddy.

No, the world has changed, and even countries better known for their free-thinking than Dhurgastan are no longer eager to welcome foreigners who want to preach whatever is the latest evangelistic creed.

I disagree with closing borders to ideas or regulating the media. If free trade works for products then I should hope it would for thoughts; the truth must win out. But I can sympathize. The knee-jerk reaction of plenty of North Americans is hostile when they hear that the Buddhists are coming from Japan to our shores, or that Saudi oil money is building mosques in Dallas. Ironically, the reaction is just as unfriendly when we learn that the Christian churches of Korea and Nigeria are sending missionaries our way.

Nationalism is on the rise everywhere. It can be a potent motive for some of mankind's best and many of its worst actions. Colonialism died of natural causes; imperialism is comatose; and communism had rigor mortised. While nationalism is on the rise everywhere, it remains to be seen what mood it has risen in.

Dhurgastanis, as a general rule, suffer the effects of a crippling inferiority complex. "Oh sure, *he* can do it. That's because he is from your country . . . or from Europe . . . or China." It leaves them a small people with small thoughts. They could do with a dose of good patriotism; not the "love it or leave it" sort, but the kind that makes a Libyan want Libya to be the best it can be and has no ax to grind with Sudan or Morocco. Let the Sudanese be the best that they can be as well.

As borders close, missionaries have become a cross section of the Church. Like a jury in an American courtroom, everybody is becoming eligible. Laymen are boarding more tramp steamers bound for distant continents than the clerics are these days. The kingdom of Heaven is relying more and more upon amateur theologians; and, though this brings attending dangers, we can remember that this is how Christian missions began in the first place.

The excuse of having no skill with which to serve overseas is beginning to ring hollow. If one does not want to serve overseas, that is fine. It has never been a requirement. But just say so, don't hide behind your profession or lack of one. Most anyone able to read this book is also licensed to operate a file cabinet or to do any of another thousand unromantic and necessary tasks.

Our group in Dhurgastan, like most mission agencies, was made up of young couples. Some wise guy in Bhadrapur did his arithmetic and discovered to our chagrin that the Mission's birthrate was actually greater than Dhurgastan's, which we were encouraging to slow down.

We were also singles. Like Christian work in all countries and during all ages, that in Dhurgastan was founded on the sacrifice and hard work of single women. There were four single women to every single man; odds that likely caused a decision for service a second or third term by a woman to be a decision to forego marriage (there are of course exceptions to this).

We were also retired people, turned out to pasture (and if I may mix my metaphors) with plenty of tread left. The puttering grayheads added wisdom and efficiency to the organization. One fragile-looking Mennonite from Toronto sat with me at lunch as she waited to go to the airport to leave Dhurgastan. She had been working at her denomination's mission board for thirty years without having ever left Canada. This had seemed dishonorable to her in some fashion and she had, therefore, come to Asia and performed miracles in our business office that no one else had been able to accomplish. Now she was returning and intended to tell her aging friends that "she has done her time and it is their turn to go."

"Their turn to go . . ." What a wonderful attitude. Think of how much of the world's sufferings could be addressed if all Christians thought similarly.

Short-term commitments

There will always be a necessity for some workers to make a career of serving in a foreign land, of living out their adult years in one culture. But the trend in missions is for people to think in shorter term commitments; for example, after fifteen years as an Australian bureaucrat to take a year's sabbatical and come over to "do one's turn" by teaching English as a second language to medical students.

We were engineers who could not help ourselves, encountering on any day's bus ride things that screamed to be paved, improved, spanned and electrified. The Scandinavians were especially bad, a lot of hyperactive, overachieving beavers who felt an uncontrollable compulsion to dam any trickle of running water and to squeeze out of it every last kilovolt.

Everyone knows that it has long been acceptable for a missionary to also be a doctor, and Christians were doing twenty percent of the health care of Dhurgastan; but that also means physical therapists, laboratory technicians, pharmacists, specialists in repairing medical equipment, nurses, administrators and midwives.

We taught at just about every level and in every conceivable subject. Teachers in the formal setting of primary and secondary schools, teacher training at the university, but less formally, literacy was taught around smoky lanterns throughout the dark, windy hills—groups learning about hygiene and kitchen gardens as they learned to recognize their alphabet. We taught nurses how to change the sheets with a patient still lying in the bed; we taught secretaries to type on the unwieldy Basha typewriters.

And the learning required artists and photographers and computer specialists to devise and design, layout, print and publish all of the posters, flash cards, pamphlets, textbooks and videos to teach about everything from leprosy to how to store grain so that the rats do not get their unfair share.

We also taught ourselves. People had to oversee the orientation of the neophytes, and someone else has to insure that they got a decent chance of learning enough Basha to get by. And it does precious little good to attract a top-notch surgeon, to orient him and give him the language if he returns to his home country after eleven months out of fear for his children's education. At one point our most desperate personnel need was for tutorial teachers for the children of the Mission's workers. Some agencies remain short-sighted and refuse to support such tutorial teachers. Those posts seem far removed from the grass roots needs of the native Dhurgastanis, when, in fact, these support posts are as essential for the work as the headquarter's staff of the sending agency itself.

We taught technology of every stripe and caliber: how to read a thermometer, to galvanize pipe and to repair shortwave radios. Twenty-some-odd percent of the nation's apples rotted out in Western Dhurgastan before they could find themselves a market. Someone in appropriate technology designed a hand-cranked apple peeler/corer that could do nine apples a minute in a wondrous polka. A machinist took the design and forged it into steel and aluminum. A food technologist taught the farmers in the West how to use the unlikely looking gadget and how to solar dry the results. Then he took their production and the heads of their cooperative in to Rajdhani to establish a beachhead at the back doors of the big tourist hotels.

Such vast effort, with so many consequences and so very little of it involving a pith-helmeted stereotype.

The dreaded social gospel? The slippery slope into liberalism? A creeping liberation theology?

I am not convinced that laymen creep or slide into heresy any more readily than their ordained brethren. If the truth be known, wrong belief often begins first in the pulpit, too far removed from the needs of real life.

Dear Friends,

An expectant world lies hushed, governments fidget behind their desks, stock exchangers around the globe gaze anxiously into their computer screens . . . but still Joanne is uncooperative and our first baby, due any moment, has not been born. If you are to hear from us this month I cannot wait any longer but must dash this off to you. You'll have to wait with the rest of them until next month to get the news.

People Don't Like to Talk to Me: I am busy, using my waiting time here in Rajdhani to prepare for the animal health courses that I have to teach in under three weeks. The language teachers find my case a profoundly disturbing one and my vocabulary obscene. I can barely stammer a comprehensible "hello" and yet I can wax eloquent on such disgusting subjects as footrot and liver abscesses.

Something Odd Is Going on Here: What a contrast; it

leaves me gasping like a mullet in the sand when I consider it! The Concorde, the world's fastest commercial airplane, spent two days this week in Rajdhani; and it caused a sensation. A group of German tycoons had rented it for an intimate round-the-world spree.

This morning, as I memorized the day's vocabulary (anemia, tapeworm, convulsion), we heard a stupendous roar and rushed into the garden of the guesthouse in time to see it thunder off into the hazy skies. It can be in Hong Kong in a matter of hours, though that short ride would set you back several thousand dollars. . . . But just over those near hills, only a hard day's walk from where I'm comfortably sitting, the daily wage for backbreaking labor in the sun is forty cents. Farmers are barely raising enough calories to keep their families skinny in the dry season; about half the children under five are dying preventable deaths.

Something disturbing is going on around here. Something about the layout of the whole place feels like a mirror image; everything looks natural enough yet somehow backwards at the same instant. A quiet voice tries to insist over the pain and hubbub, "But I'm sure that it wasn't intended to be this way." People eating their no-cholesterol oat bran at the breakfast table are frightened into buying an alarm system by the evil leering at them from the newsprint. Even worse is the evil only they know which exists within, oat bran or no. An ogre outside batters at the crumbling walls blow after heavy blow; and as if that isn't bad enough, somebody keeps letting down the drawbridge from the inside.

The Fall of man is no myth, if by that you mean some harmless children's tale invented to account for something inexplicable. There is nothing harmless about it at all. It is more horrible to contemplate than death camps, mass graves and birth defects. We can be dismayed, but we are silly to be surprised. Jesus and the apostles frequently forewarned us: "Beloved, do not think it strange concerning the fiery trial which is to try you, as though some strange thing happened to you." There is war going on in high places. We hear the echo of distant artillery; sometimes a shell shrieks by and crashes nearby, causing senseless slaughter.

But forewarned and explained are not the same as complacent. "You must endure hardship as a good soldier of Jesus Christ." Those are our orders. Of course everyone must rest and get away from the trenches awhile; but duty is duty and obedience is joy. If the guns sound too distant for too long maybe you had better think about returning to the front; at least don't consider a quiet situation as normal.

Your partner,
Martin

CHAPTER 11

Did the Apostles Play Golf?

The Missionary and Free Time

"We have to feel the universe at once an ogre's castle,
to be stormed, and yet as our own cottage, to which
we can return at evening."

G.K. Chesterton

Dear Friends,

As I write to you I find myself in unusual surroundings, sitting in a quiet study among deep armchairs and weighty books, a moment of welcome relief from the past eighteen months and their dirth of quiet moments. *Cracks around the Foundation*: Wives know more about these things. Dummy me did not recognize in myself the grim symptoms: the short temper, listless insomnia, a restless apathy. It finally occurred to me that Joanne might be correct in her estimation one day when a small, village boy was out hunting birds with his sling shot and one of his stones ripped up through the branches and then clattered at my feet. Without an instant's hesitation, I whipped around picked up the stone and sent it zinging back at the little boy. I'm sure that my intention was not to maim, but most definitely I meant to make contact. Thank goodness that my aim is bad.

I needed a vacation.

The Great Haggis Tour: Well, our plans changed like a housewife trying to decide where to put the new piano. She dithers as the burly movers huff and heave. In the end we bumped into ourselves boarding a Lufthansa flight bound for Great Britain.

Wonderful people who had never met us (friends of friends of colleagues in Dhurgastan) have kept us in their homes; an ideal way to see the country and to get to know the people. One can sightsee all day and then come home in the evening and ask one's hosts all of the questions that the sights have generated. Now, after two hectic weeks negotiating British traffic in a car rented from an agency that deals only with furloughing missionaries, we have the use of a tremendous Scottish house near the Western coast in Ayrshire. It is a wonderful house that seems confused in its ambitions: staircases lead to the oddest landings and at unexpected levels, one stumbles upon cozy studies and large living areas. It cannot seem to make up its mind whether to be homey or grand. Its owners are friends of a colleague who teaches in Bhadrapur and are themselves off vacationing somewhere.

Our days are the perfect blend of lounging and playing with dear friends from Texas who have joined us in Scotland and shall then fly back to spend a month with us in Dhurgastan. I've had the opportunity to speak in churches wherever we have been each Sunday.

Vacation But Not Retirement: We have enjoyed several great moments on this trip; some of them have even felt symbolic in the way that we always expect real life to be after we have read a good novel; only it never is. Like the time we were standing among the ruins of Hadrian's

Wall (a huge stone defense built across the entire width of the island by the Romans as an effort to deter the enthusiasms of the warlike Scots). As we contemplated the scene and tried to imagine the ruins whole once more, a fighter-bomber of the RAF rushed over us at real-life, tree-top level. It was silent as a cloud until directly overhead, and then the blast of sound knocked our friend's toddler flat out in the dark green English grass. And it occurred to me, "My, how things have changed through the centuries." But after a second moment's thought, "Then again, maybe they haven't changed at all."

Another time we were driving into the coastal city of Ayre to do some shopping, and on the way we bypassed Irvine in a sweep of highway. On the horizon there appeared to be an impressive church. Nothing surprising in that; tiny Scotland bristles with the gray spires of Presbyterian churches. But this one hinted at something even more imposing than usual, and I wanted a closer look.

I still cannot decide whether I like or detest that church. It is rather a deformity, built in the same neo-rococo style, or whatever it is that the awful ornate courthouse in Waxahachie, Texas, was done in. As one approached, there was the strange sensation that the building shrank in perspective rather than growing because the architect had known well how to dupe his audience. It was actually much smaller than one would have guessed. It really served as only an excuse to build a fantastic steeple and an enormous rose window worthy of a major cathedral; the rest of the structure was dwarfish and underdeveloped. It seemed like a great, barrel-chested muscleman dangling shriveled legs from his wheelchair.

I snapped some slides of it (I confess to being one of those bores who loves photos of old churches), and then I stepped around to get the name of the church.

It came as a nasty shock: "Trinity Centre" was no longer a church. It was, instead, "meeting rooms for let." A dance studio, a day-care center—no one could decide on an effective use of the main sanctuary and so it remained empty. The front doors were locked and spray-painted with graffiti. Trash blew about the unkempt grounds.

If Jesus delays His return for another thousand years, will there be faith on earth?

The East is unaware. The West is unconcerned. And I cannot, for the life of me, decide which is worse.

Your partner,
Martin

The problem of vacations

Do missionaries deserve vacations? They get paid to live in exotic places that the rest of us only dream of as we flip through the travel magazines at the barber shop. Worse yet, that pay comes from the donations of those of us waiting our turn in the barber shop. Don't they feel guilty, surrounded as they are by such horrible poverty, to take out time for needless hobbies? Can a missionary afford free time?

Those questions occur to the missionaries themselves, at least I know that they did to me; but ironically, our entire mission in Dhurgastan began as a needless hobby. The country was closed to foreign influence for one and a half centuries. The one exception was the British consul and his family that were allowed residence in Rajdhani; otherwise, contact was effectively forbidden. During that one hundred and fifty years Christian missions made great advances in both India and China, but Dhurgastan remained uncontacted, a dark rock rising above a rising tide. Not, however, that the nation went unnoticed; several Australian missionaries, assigned to positions in Northern India, continued to look past their work and over the border into the untouched hills.

The first missionaries entered Dhurgastan on visas permitting them to bird watch, of all unlikely projects. And yet it was not so very unlikely: Dhurgastan was known to be home to many rare species and the two Australian men had taken to the sport during their years in India. But as they tramped about and scanned the trees with their binoculars, could they help themselves if they noticed other things as well, like a spot just perfect to build a new hospital?

Going back to India, they stopped in Rajdhani and met with the prime minister. In those days visitors were so infrequent that such an audience was easily obtained. They explained about the location in Bhind, how there was not a health facility within six-days' walk in any direction, and about their organization's willingness to rectify this grievous situation.

And so began the Dhurgastan International Mission: hospitals brought schools and schools brought agriculturalists who needed engineers. To this day, bird watching is less a hobby than an obligatory rite within the organization. The entire group gathers from the remote nooks and crannies of Dhurgastan once a year, and at the conference we feast ourselves on fellowship and Bible teaching in English, which over the months we have all so dreadfully missed. We come in to eat and relax behind the walls of the university campus which we borrow for an entire week during the holidays. Does this mean that we greedily take advantage of the unheard of opportunity to sleep late? Not for a moment. No, before the sun has climbed over the far side of the hills whole crowds of us arise and are out birding. It's our tradition. The Mission newsletter mentions the name of anyone who sights their three hundredth species.

The need for hobbies

Missionary life, especially in a group as diverse and cosmopolitan as ours, is also given to stamp collecting: you had never intended on indulging in it, you were not sure exactly when it started, but there it was.

I did not make it through my first week in the guesthouse in Rajdhani before I had contracted the condition. Lovely stamps from Hong Kong and Ecuador arrived on the envelopes addressed to my new friends; and you found yourself trading them across the dinner table.

"What, this old thing? Why, it's our most common stamp; but sure, if you would like it, please take it."

But these were the sunny days, the first innocent steps onto a dismal staircase that spiraled ever downward toward ruin and disgrace. Informal swapping soon was not enough to satisfy the craving for new acquisitions: what was needed was an organized system. Clubs were formed. I must confess to have been personally involved in two such round-robin groups. A tattered, foot-sore envelope would arrive in one's mailbox every month or two, and one would take it home and go through it carefully, weighing the various merits of the stamps inside. After choosing those ten that most caught your eye, you replenished the stock with ten of your useless duplicates, sealed the envelope and sent it on to the next name down the list. With time, however, even such arrangements were not enough for the voracious stamp albums; this way you merely picked through the discards of others, you needed a direct source, new releases.

A hardcore philatelist is a dangerous, anti-social animal; and here we were, a community peopled almost wholly by such beasts. No length was too far, no stunt too brazen to outdo the competition. The best one that I knew of was the case of Willem, a devious Dutch teacher in Katihar. He managed to have himself appointed the project mail person, which was no great feat considering that he was also the project manager.

One of the mail person's duties was to sort the mail and to put it into everyone's individual boxes. Ah, you begin to see his game, do you? It was dirty pool. This way he intercepted even the mail of fellow collectors from his "upstream" position. His justification ran something as follows: envelopes and packages already arrive in Hatibar in such a rumpled state, who will mind if I take a scalpel and carefully, ever so carefully, remove the stamps (oh, just a few) from the corners?

Well, Willem's collection quickly outpaced all of the others'. It is a difficult thing to confront one's boss over the removal of a stamp or two (remember these are missionaries with which we are dealing). But tardy as it was, the day of reckoning came when the entire project rose in revolt. The government did not topple; Willem retained his post as mail person, but concessions were made: no more stamps would be removed without permission. Even so, every once in a while, one would get an envelope that had gotten the best of Willem, and in a discreet hand next to the address would be penciled, "Should you be interested, I do not possess this stamp."

Missionaries and computers

Computers have, of course, reached even the mission field; and they pull their weight as tools for translation, controlling medical inventories, coordinating libraries and designing suspension bridges in an unstable land prone to earthquakes. They also have a powerful appeal to a certain type of personality; and although they vehemently deny it, the machines become another needless hobby.

The subtle advantage of the hackers over the philatelists is that we nonenthusiasts cannot actually tell when it is that we are performing some vital task and saving great gobs of time by doing it on the machine, or when we are only indulging ourselves in our fascination, taking twice as long as we would with a ruler and three rubber bands.

Bupto was the Mission's most remote project. There was no road leading to it, and its elevation was enough that snow prevented flights for several months each winter. The feeling of isolation told on the expatriots, and the place had a bad reputation among us as a good place to have a nervous breakdown. The lifestyle was more of a grind because produce was not available; one had to cook on firewood instead of kerosene, and this meant arranging contracts with the locals, notorious for their dishonesty. It was a backward place even for a backward country.

There were five families assigned to Bupto, helping to construct, administer and teach a large technical school that was meant to be part of the government's ambitious scheme of practical training. Dhurgastan needs education, but in the hands-on, turn-a-wrench kind of school, rather than the theoretical, academic setting of a university.

There were five families in Bupto and six personal computers. How that situation came to be I cannot imagine. Oh sure, there are reasons given for the anomaly. There are text books to be word-processed, but no one has the nerve to admit, "Hey, I've fallen in love with these nifty machines, and it's my hobby."

The hobby of walking

A land as picturesque and deprived of roads as Dhurgastan makes great walkers of almost every one of its inhabitants, and it is a useful hobby to acquire when one is going by necessity to spend so much time doing it. Work required it of us: making a slow circuit of the village in an adult literacy program, my follow-up trips to visit the animal health trainees whose house might simply be four hours up the valley from the landing strip. When vacation time arrived, one merely put on a good pair of shoes and walked someplace new and saw a different valley or went to visit missionary friends in another project. We had sixty-year-old women who, after thirty-five years in the country, could take a youthful new arrival out on a Saturday's jaunt and walk him into a stupor.

Walking is a friendly, neighborly hobby that invites others to join in and brings, along with its pack lunch, many interesting opportunities. One English friend, very prim and speaking with an extremely posh Cambridge accent, was a first-rate walker; and in her knapsack she always included a few gospels or Christian books. When the sudden storms of the hills sent us all scurrying into a wayside tea shop, as the rest of us chattered to each other, my friend would pull up a stool, sip daintily at her tea and read one of her books.

It was not long at all before the locals, also driven in for protection from the rain, were asking her how she came to be able to read in Basha. One thing followed another, and soon she was selling her books to her new acquaintances. She sold the books, she told me, because it made it more likely that they would be read; free literature gathers dust.

Then there was Stoney, a great walker in her own right, but famous for taking along her two Border Collies, Jake and Jenny. Up early every morning they had a hike before returning to a heavy day's schedule at the boarding school where, as the dogs slept beneath her desk, Stoney taught math and literature. Between classes or on the morning walks the two dogs earned their reputation by retrieving a rubber ball cratered with exuberant teeth marks. Nothing had ever been seen like it. The persecuted village curs had no reason to cooperate in such a game; and the Dhurgastanis would watch the dogs run after the ball and bring it back as if the process were magic.

Whatever the chosen hobby, it was necessary that it not require a great deal of complicated gear. Even flying a kite out on a raw March wind was enough to attract an enormous crowd of spectators who, in their enthusiasm to help and take part, were likely to shred the kite or turn its precious string into a Gordian knot.

Getting away

Our project in Bhadrapur, being on the tourist trail, offered much more sophisticated choice of what to do with our time when duty was not insistently calling. Down at Lakeside, a thirty-minute taxi ride away and reason for the tourist trail, were clusters of tiny guesthouses and their associated restaurants, dozens of them, boasting both atmosphere and cuisine unimaginable.

Here one could find hot showers and Mexican food. A man operated two small sailboats. He had never been in a sailboat himself but had built them from pictures in a magazine that a tourist had left in his lodge. They plowed through the water like a badger does loose soil; but still, pretty remarkable all things considered.

The spinach quiche and vermicelli recipes must have been learned from photographs as well because, though they looked the scrumptious real McCoy, they all managed to taste like curry.

It was the cheesecake or the apple crumble at a little place called the Hungry Eye that always caught me. Western music beckoned a passersby from the street; and, even though you knew better from a hundred disappointments, you would order one of the luscious desserts in the big front window, hoping this time would be different. Alas, curried sawdust again that looks like something off the pages of *Good Housekeeping*.

Lakeside was a magnificent mistake of tangled cultures. Acapulco or Monaco or Las Vegas cannot provide more weirdness in a classic setting. Not Western, and by no means Dhurgastani, it was a strange bubble in space and time that operated under its own laws of nature. In the mid-seventies it had been the end of the international hippie trail (drugs could be had at a bargain basement rate); and after trying everything everywhere else, the burned-out flower children crash-landed around its shores.

The missionaries all discovered their favorite restaurants despite the fact that food and service were in reality the same at all of them. But one wants familiar surroundings in which to while away a lazy Sunday afternoon, away from the village, drinking the instant Nescafe from India which served for coffee in every one of the favorite spots. There was the Baba Lodge, Richard's chosen hangout, where one could buy the best and the worst fish in the country, and there was no way to know beforehand which it was going to be on any given Sunday. The Snowlands was the place to find the Barclay's, up on its balcony or in the back room where the walls were plastered with posters of heavy metal groups that had thankfully broken up years earlier. The Don't Cross Me By was Stoney's spot, or sometimes for variety she frequented the Paradise Hotel and Kontinental Eatery. Down at the Kantipur if one mentioned that he was an acquaintance of Ken's (bursar at the boarding school) there was a fifteen percent discount. I could never discover what Ken had done to earn such respect, but the tradition continued for years after he had returned to London.

The missionaries were an insignificant minority amid the sea of foreigners who came from every continent. Kids from North America flirted with others from Europe, and there were more and more business-minded Japanese holiday makers peopling the little terraces and the round tables with the tablecloths, once white, that were now turned into maps from seasons of spilled coffee and the splatters from sizzling steaks. That's right! Beef could even be obtained at Lakeside, but in deference to local sensitivities, it was referred to as "filet."

Talk was a babble of accents, English usually being spoken as the *lingua franca*. They poured over maps together in anticipation of their treks, or they sported ten-day beards and infected blisters, boasting of their daring exploits out in the mountains.

Part of me despised Lakeside, with its Tibetan tourist trinkets and its stalls of used paperbacks purchased at the Frankfurt airport. I vainly spoke to the waiters in Basha to show them that I was not one of these commoners. But another side of me enjoyed the crazy pastiche of East and West. It was fun to be able to argue changes in the European Community with a Swiss gymnastics instructor after a long two weeks of teaching hill farmers about the life cycle of roundworms and the need for toilets.

The need for leisure

I have not, however, been answering our questions but have skirted the issue with brief examples of what we did. What then is the purpose of free time? God, after all, invented it with His sabbath.

Leisure can be overdone, no doubt about it. I have seen too many good people suddenly age and lose interest because they could not handle the leisure that came with retirement. This extreme conceded, we can move on to the vast majority of humanity. People do need small increments of relaxing change, especially those in professions like air-traffic controllers, obstetricians and missionaries, people who operate under the continuous tension of one crisis after another. A missionary is, by nature and by job description, constantly giving of himself to others, trying to help even when help is not appreciated. There must be times to refill and refresh the body and the spirit, quiet opportunities for families to let down their guard, chances for God to speak again.

Out in a remote posting, one is often one's own supervisor, the top of the heap in the immediate vicinity; it is easy, therefore, to pamper oneself and come in late or go home early. Who's to know?

I have known one or two people who were, in my judgment, bad apples; people who were missionaries by default because they were afraid to go home and to compete in their own cultures. What could they do if they went back? No, thank you. We've carved out a nice little niche for ourselves here and are in for the duration.

These were the ones who abused their responsibilities and

frittered away too much of their time on diversions. They were, in fact, killing time until they could retire.

It is not good medicine, however, to kill one's patient with a treatment to save them from a particular disease; and in comparison with the few bad apples, I have known many missionaries who as a matter of policy worked themselves into an early furlough and returned to their own country frazzled and shell-shocked. And I have known of mission boards that unintentionally encouraged too much work.

It was my friend Liston-Pym who envied me my hobby—taking theology courses by correspondence. In my situation, when my spiritual diet was being served up in a foreign language, these courses came as a great joy to me. But Gerard explained to me that, though he would like to do some similar studies, it was out of the question. His mission would not understand, would see it as an infallible indication that he had too much time on his hands, time that should be devoted either to work or to the local congregation.

His mission had a point; time with Dhurgastanis outside of office hours should be maximized. We could not go home every evening and simply pursue our entertainment. But the point, taken too far (and how far is too far varies between us) is a recipe for disaster. My friend needed an enjoyable outlet, be it stamps or artificial intelligence or patristic church history.

One last warning: spare time must be chaperoned so that it does not degenerate into "coffee and complaining." People take odd solace in dwelling upon their miserable lot in life, and, as always, missionaries are more like normal people than normal people like to admit.

I have sat (and participated) in some massive, communal self-pity sessions. Without an outlet, the bilge water just collects into a stagnant pond and produces nothing except unpleasant odors. The Dhurgastanis can smell, too; and we must be careful lest such aromas taint the wonders of the gospel. Better to vent the dirty accumulations through collecting butterflies or pressing flowers, writing bad poetry or learning the recorder.

What about the needs around us? How can I go inside and listen to cassettes from home when people are malnourished?

I had another friend, one who took such questions seriously. For him this was no rhetorical matter. He could not bear to see anyone unhappy; and seeing the need, in his case, constituted the call to be the one to answer it. He considered hyperactivity the most essential ingredient of a missionary's profile and would run about, juggling as many plates at once as possible—settings for four, eight . . . twelve, teacups and all.

He got a lot done; no doubt of that, but at tremendous cost; and it was only a matter of time until his account was overdrawn. Family tensions, health breaking down, colleagues getting irritated with his ever-present helping nose.

Someone finally loaded, took careful aim and gave it to him—both barrels. "No one, including you, is indispensable."

A new, painful concept for my friend and not a moment too soon. It burned his fingers and blackened an eye, I suppose; but it also acted to slow his pace sufficiently to keep him able to serve overseas—the steady burn of a lantern rather than the searing flash of the meteorite that is, "Ooh, so bright!" Poof and it's gone.

CHAPTER 12

The Sulphur Burps

Missionaries and Their Health

"Whilst my Physitians by their love are growne
Cosmographers, and I their Mapp . . . "

John Donne

It is not long into any consideration of going overseas before one is concerned with a grisly list of vaccines that are rare and hard to obtain. There are fears of unknown microbes carried by devilishly tricky mosquitoes and memories of Uncle Jack's fiasco of a honeymoon down in Puerto Vallarta.

There is, in fact, wholesale confusion on the subject of God's will and disease. The definite answer is certainly beyond my poor abilities; nevertheless, I have spent a lot of time pondering it and have seen my share of creatures die. Daring to offer no answer, I do not hesitate to offer a few observations.

When Joanne was diagnosed as having a particular cancer, our best friends in college ran to the library and looked it up. With tears in their eyes they read that her chances were poor; this was the greatest killer of Americans between the ages of nineteen and thirty-one. Happily, they had made a minor error—they had read a ten-year-old text on the subject, and in one decade things had radically improved. Treatment was now much more effective, and the physicians were more confident in their regimens. If you had to have cancer, this was now the one to have.

Another woman, a trusted friend of the family and someone who had played a vital role in my becoming a Christian in the first place, had a completely different reaction to our devastating news. She sat us down and strongly advised in no uncertain terms, that Joanne refrain from taking any treatment. Was not our God, she reasoned, able to heal us of all of our infirmities?

She gave this advice to us in all sober charity and selfless concern. She also proved herself true to the concept, for when later her son began to evince the signs of encroaching schizophrenia, she again preferred to entrust the handling of the situation to God's hand rather than the efforts of puny human doctors.

But something happened which gave me pause to reconsider the whole issue, for up until then I had considered myself a rank failure in my allowing, even insisting, that Joanne receive therapy. The same friend with the great faith was also a great gardener, and one afternoon she managed with her new pruning shears to snip off the end of her thumb. Pandemonium ensued and she was, quite rightly, off to the emergency room for stitches and a bandage like a rabbit shot from a cannon.

Shameless hypocrisy? It seemed so at first; but then I realized that, after her own fashion, she was consistent. Her theology and her medicine were comfortable with one another's habits, like an old married couple. There was an unspoken, and probably unconscious, guiding principle that was at work in her thinking. If a condition was obvious to the unaided eye, if it involved an undeniable physical cause, if it did not require one to rely upon tests and chemistry beyond her understanding, in such a case one could resort to physicians. If, on the other hand, the layman could not see the problem without a lot of medical high tech wizardry, then the matter was of spiritual warfare and something best confronted by prayer. Resorting to physicians in this second case was actually counterproductive because a lack of faith robbed prayer of its efficacy.

Sprained ankles, broken toes, a cut lip—these were obviously the jurisdiction of the local general practitioner. Cancer, mental illness and, one would assume, heart disease were problems requiring faith instead of treatments. One's own headache (as opposed to someone else's) poses a nasty gray area. But I am convinced that were her son's schizophrenia to have caused him to break out in an unsightly purple rash, she would have speedily taken him to see a dermatologist.

This dear woman, lest I have made her sound so, is neither stupid nor negligently wicked. She is confident that a loving God's will could only be the perfect health of all His servants. She would undoubtedly give nodding assent to the "germ theory," but in cases of unseen disease would believe the microbes to be the unwitting agents of Satanic forces. (The book of Job indicates that Satan can cause human disease; but it falls far short of teaching that he is the cause of all ailments.)

My observation is that most missionaries would disagree with my dear friend: their overseas experience teaches that God can heal, and yet He does not always; that His servants do fall prey to any number of uncomfortable conditions; that being ill does not prove one's faith to be too weak.

Those ugly "tummy disorders"

Giardia is a pernicious little flagellate that prefers, all things being equal, to live in the large intestine of hapless people. In this unlikely neighborhood, it cavorts and frolics, blowing horrible hydrogen sulfide bubbles which the sufferer can taste in the form of a "sulphur burp." The incubation period, that is the time from which you ingest your first giardia until the first symptoms are apparent, is about ten days to two weeks.

I had been in Dhurgastan for about fifteen days when, while sitting downstairs at the table, I said that I did not care for any breakfast. My face carried a distasteful grimace which my host could hardly help noticing, and in answer to his question I replied that I kept belching rotten eggs.

My host, normally a compassionate enough fellow, could not help himself but smile knowingly.

The infection acted as a sort of badge of membership. I had arrived. The next time that I was in a group of missionaries and they began trading stories on tummy troubles (and they invariably do when gathered in a group) I could claim the status of initiate. Such sessions of "bowel talk" are a constant part of missionary life, taking the place, I suppose, of the sports scores which they do without in their foreign exile.

Dhurgastan is famed for such tummy disorders, and they become a part of everyone's life, rather like rainy days. From being unmentionable (and yet polite for bowel talk), diarrhea becomes a way of life, and one learns to redefine that ugly word.

We were spared the ravages of malaria, but we had quite enough in the way of typhoid, tuberculosis, meningitis, hepatitis and numerous and sundry fevers of unknown origin.

Everyone is sick more frequently than they were used to at home. And twisted up in sweaty sheets keeping time by the pounding of one's temples, black frustration follows wolf-like on the stumbling heels of every bout with illness. One cannot shake the taunting idea that if "I weren't in Dhurgastan this wouldn't be happening to me."

More than likely you're right. Dhurgastan is a filthy place, and any minor cut can easily mean an abscess and swollen lymph nodes in two or three days.

And as pesky as the fevers and the infections are, these are actually the most pleasant of the conditions. There are others that bring worse torments with them.

Elspeth, a British veterinarian, used to put it this way, "If you have a crack in your armor, Dhurgastan will find and exploit it." She had reason to make that statement. I arrived in Bhadrapur after a terrible journey on a night bus. In order to not arrive before the city taxis were operating, they stopped the bus frequently at tea shops to drink and to play a few hands of cards. It kept us in a zombied state between sleep and consciousness. But, eager to set the pace and to show people who they were dealing with in me, after breakfast at my new supervisor's house, I was off to my new office. There, however, I was informed that Elspeth had left for Rajdhani on the night bus the evening before. We passed each other somewhere in the moonlit hills. She was going in mentally exhausted and depressed, and later I was instructed by the counselors in the Mission that under no circumstances was I to trouble her with any questions concerning our program.

I was devastated. What it meant was that my transition period of overlap with her was obliterated, vaporized, rendered nonexistent. Here are the keys, find your way. Don't call us; and we won't call you.

An observant counselor had actually been on top of the problem early on when in one of our annual health forms with which the Mission troubles us, Elspeth had ticked the box indicating a recent change in sleeping habits.

She was an extremely competent veterinarian, and had a good command of Basha; nevertheless, she acted the unsavory part of her own worst enemy, with nothing but criticism of herself and her abilities. The constant strain of cross-cultural life had worn on her like Chinese water torture. Tiny drops (drip, drip, drip); nothing at all over which to be concerned (Drip, Drip, Drip); don't be foolish, this isn't anything major (DRIP, DRIP, DRIP)—until she could cope with it no longer.

There had been one major setback amid the numerous little niggling hassles when a good friend of hers, a doctor who was working with orphans, came down with hepatitis. Modern medicine can offer little help with this viral disease; bed rest is palliative. It can be months before someone recovers enough to perform at their full capacity. But Elspeth's friend was all but alone in her work with the children. As she became more and more fatigued, others would plead with her to rest; but always came her reply, "And if I'm in bed who is going to take care of these poor little ones?"

Who indeed?

An ailing liver, however, is not an organ with which to argue; it cares nothing for urgent schedules or essential responsibilities. The woman continued the debate and her condition deteriorated until it was serious. Elspeth now saw that it was her duty to act decisively, and she took the doctor and forced her onto an airplane bound for Great Britain. The woman had to recuperate, and she would not do so as long as she remained in Dhurgastan.

Elspeth's firm resolve was absolutely the right course to follow; sadly, however, she had remained polite for too long. Things had progressed too far, and her friend died before she arrived home.

Such a tragic, needless death brings with its cargo of sorrow whole barges filled with guilt and doubt. Why didn't I act more quickly instead of listening to her? Anyone with any sense would have seen that she had to be made to rest. How could God let one of His ministers be so fruitlessly sacrificed? Where is there one shred of sense and glory in that?

Such grief turned the niggling hassles of everyday life into burning needles. Elspeth kept things to herself; and, though she lost her sense of humor, she was not one to complain about anything except herself. Times of depression followed. Thereafter, if one wanted to see Elspeth display a fiery anger, all one had to do was to appear overly self-sacrificial for the sake of "the work."

She managed to complete her term, which is important psychologically. People who have to return home early, even for the most urgent of reasons, arrive there dragging in their luggage a dead corpse: the image of the "failed missionary."

Mental and physical anguish blur and blend like watercolors applied when the paper is still wet. Nice, neat boundaries fade.

Other causes of mental stress

We had a horticulture student from New Zealand come to Dhurgastan on a year-long project studying bamboo and its potential uses to slow down erosion of the farmer's soil. He was living with a missionary family down in the bazaar when he was not traveling about gathering experience with his precious bamboo.

About halfway through his time, his host family began to mention odd behavior on his part. He grew more reclusive—but they chalked it up to a young man's reaction to acute homesickness and culture shock. He began to spend whole days in his dark room sitting in a cane-backed chair, just sitting. Finally he would not communicate, refused meals and would not come out.

It was obvious to the project that he was undergoing a major mental disorder unlike the periodic depression common to many missionaries. We put him aboard a bus for Rajdhani and informed a psychiatrist who worked in the mission hospital there.

She did something that had never occurred to any of the rest of us. Though he had never complained of a fever, she took his temperature and found it to be elevated. She quickly recognized his problem to be typhoid, a manic form that affects one's thinking and personality. He was hospitalized and put on antibiotics.

His behavior had been so strange that some in the project were contemplating exorcism for the case. It had seemed to have no physical cause to account for his rapid decline.

After a full recovery he had dinner with Joanne and me and told us of his unusual experience. To all outside observers he had appeared depressed and unresponsive to stimulation; but he told us, however, that this perception was incorrect. Actually, the whole while his consciousness had been heightened and his brain was working at a feverish pace. He seemed to have total recall, remembering all that he had ever heard or read; and as he sat there statue-like in his chair, in reality he was dealing with frenzied thoughts that bounced about inside his head like raquetballs. As he got better, friends would visit him in his hospital room; and he told us that on several occasions he spoke to them for six hours straight without interruption, not allowing them the comfort of even one word. He simply talked and talked and talked, able to quote lengthy passages of the Scriptures without the slightest effort.

God can and does heal. I say this not to tip my hat politely to orthodox supernaturalism, but out of real conviction. The Dhurgastani church is filled with converts first convinced by a miraculous healing. I have known a missionary in a remote station who operated a clinic with little more than aspirin and prayer. She would tell you herself with a smile that she did not rely very much on the aspirin. We saw people healed through surgery and proper use of medicines. Sadly, I also witnessed people dying of tuberculosis because they had defaulted on their treatments. They needed the medicine for nine months but had stopped for some very lame reason, after three.

The matter is mysterious and complicated, but all of life is that. Why did God create mycobacteria? I have no answer; but that doesn't surprise me too much. I do not know why God created anything in the first place. Does that cause doubts? No, I'm not bright enough to doubt—the alternatives seem to have even less sense to offer.

CHAPTER 13

The Mother Teresa Syndrome

The Weight of Correspondence

"What! with men, of all creatures, will ye have commerce?"

The Koran

There is a sword line drawn through humanity that cleaves it into two broad divisions: those who enjoy letter writing and those who do not. It is a happy convenience when a missionary falls within the ranks of those who do because, though it was careful to never appear on a job description or be included on any of those papers signed back at the home office, it is a duty that comes with the territory. Just try and ignore it.

One wants to stay in contact with relatives and friends, especially when deprived of a telephone and the chance to go to Thanksgiving dinner over at Uncle Bill's in Victoria. One needs to keep financial contributors informed and feeling appreciated. This sounds commercial and mercenary, but the Mission is quick to teach that it is godly prudence. And, unwanted mantle or not, going overseas brings with it the role of prophet and valued counselor. The missionary has a responsibility to interpret the world's needs to the church at home so that it better understands the conflict in which it has a part to play. And people—good friends, acquaintances and complete strangers—will write in search of your advice or consolation: "How do I know if I am supposed to serve overseas? What is your opinion about speaking in tongues? Should I feel guilty worrying about insurance and my retirement plan, letting them prevent me from becoming a missionary?" It is a daunting privilege to be allowed in on the secret thinking of so many people. You have to remind yourself that you are not qualified to answer most of them.

Some of it may be that a missionary acts as a distant clergy-replacement. Not as intimidating as a priest or minister; far enough away to be a low-risk confidante.

We went through, at twelve thousand miles removed, the dissolution of the marriage of one of Joanne's high school friends. They had done nothing more than exchange Christmas cards for years, but this woman needed someone upon which to unburden her anguish. We tried to help with what we considered biblical advice; but, in the end, all we could do was be a willing ear. I hope that is all that God required of us. The thing lost its hem and then completely unraveled in spite of our letters.

The importance of prayer letters

Our Mission agency asked us to write monthly "prayer letters" to the list of people interested in our efforts in Dhurgastan. The threat behind the request was that, if we fell into that half of humanity that could not make itself correspond, they would write the list for us in awful letters about our vital contribution to the efforts to relieve world hunger. Our list ran to about two hundred and fifty names, a Who's Who of your parents' friends, old college chums, former employers and names that inexplicably would just appear on our computer printouts. Mr. Gallup and his polling people could not intentionally design a more eclectic group.

We were flabbergasted by the people who became and remained regular correspondents. Was it my brother Harry? No, I did not get a letter from him for three years. Instead, it was those least expected, marginal acquaintances, people with whom you could not remember having even been on pleasant terms. People like Old Widow Babbington. We had known her at a church for one brief year during veterinary college. She began every letter with a heart-wrenching apology for writing so seldomly, never realizing that she was considered a prolific, loyal regular. We grew to recognize her little pink stationery with the handwriting that somehow managed to identify her as a grandmother.

We deeply appreciated all of our mail, although there were a few categories which caused us some discomfort. I mention these at the peril of sounding cynical, ungrateful or worse yet, blasphemous. These letters began:

> Greetings dear ones in that Name above every name, the Holiest, Highest most glorious Kingest of kings, to the Lamb slain before the foundations . . .

Imagine the guilt that we felt when, instead of a comfort or encouragement, we found such a letter an irritation. Yes, the Apostle Paul did begin his epistles in a similar vein (but with more laconic restraint), and nothing said by them was less than the absolute truth; but sitting as we were, so estranged from anything familiar, to be written to in such loquacious spirituality only added to our sense of the surreal. We craved encouragement in the Lord, but it did little good when it came like John of the Cross writing to

Teresa of Avila. It caused our sense of rootlessness to worsen. We needed something earthy and familiar dripping fewer quotes by Spurgeon and Tozer, but sporting more basketball scores—even though we never follow basketball. We wanted to be "normal," whatever that is. The air was thin at the top of so tall a pedestal and it made us wobbly. Sigh. They meant well.

Correspondence with someone in Dhurgastan is an exhortation to patience. Some colleagues were frustrated by the slow pace; I was tickled when anything arrived at all. I learned to hold long conversations with a month-long silence between replies, but there are rules to the art, most importantly when dealing with parents.

Say it is Saturday afternoon, church is over and Joanne takes a nap after fixing me a brunch of beans and rice. This is my weekly slot reserved for writing my parents. But say further that this past week I've been sick since Wednesday and am only now beginning to feel strength and the will to live returning. I want to get the health frustrations off of my chest, but caution! Consider:

1. I mention a tussle of moderate proportions with an unfriendly bacteria.
2. My parents receive the letter two weeks later (by which time I am long recovered). They immediately dash off to me a concerned question, and the offer to contact the Pentagon's Immediate Response Team to have me air-rescued.
3. I receive their anxious query two weeks later, and by this time have trouble remembering the incident to which they refer. I write a consoling missive.
4. My parents receive reassurance. But my three-day bug in the parental brain, armed as they are with

documentation and post marks, has been trans-morgrified into a six-week-long tango with the Grim Reaper.

Much better simply to write: "Dear folks—Am feeling fine, though I was ever so slightly ill for forty-five minutes briefly last Thursday. Fear not, am fully recovered. . . ."

Such slow communication requires a maturity that we lose in a society constructed around the telephone and fax machine. A voice over the microwaves can answer an ambiguity or rephrase the critical passage, but a letter lies dead and unresponsive once its message is disgorged. Asked to clarify, it merely says the same thing once more.

September 7
Dear Folks,
. . . About Harry's [my older and sole brother] spikey hair—I bet that was hard. You went to the trouble of setting up the interview and he appeared to go to the trouble of doing all that he could to scuttle a good first impression. You were ambitious for him to don a jacket and to get a position in the fledgling company. He is right—a la the 1960s—in one sense we should not care how another person's hair looks. But you are right as well—in one sense—this is not how the world operates; strangers can only go by appearances and things associated with those appearances. . . .

October 5
(in Joanne's hand):
Dear Ma and Pa,
. . . I'm sorry that we all occasionally "misinterpret" each other. We were also *both* very distressed about Harry's

having interviewed with a punk-rock haircut, and hurt for you, knowing how it disappointed you. Regarding this, Martin's letter was meant to remind you of things that you already knew & hoping that you wouldn't feel responsible for *Harry's* actions. It's hard to always be understood in letters, isn't it?—you can't just call the person up & ask what it was that they meant by that remark, you know?

October 25

Dear Folks,

. . . Dad's letter about my letter about Harry's interview (follow that?) made me realize afresh how our snail-like correspondence magnifies our chances of hurting each other's feelings inadvertently in a way that can be avoided in a face to face chat. If one reads the same words twice, only using two different tones of voice, wildly varying meanings can be had. (I suppose this accounts for how Shakespeare can be made "new" after three hundred years of heavy traffic.) I meant not to correct you, to sound disapproving or side with H. I only thought that you might benefit from a glimpse of the lesson from a mind (mine) that also grew up in the sixties. I only waste precious space on it now because a comment that Dad made sounded prematurely defensive. . . .

Communication and the crisis

My brother and his shenanigans with his hair, good grief! Other examples were not as ludicrous. A gatekeeper from the boarding school came running down the hill toward the farm one Sunday morning. These fellows were all retired out of the Indian army (India uses many Dhurgastani mercenaries, not unlike the more famous Nepali Gurkhas) and they loved to try to teach me how to salute properly, timing the stamp of my foot with a crisp snap of my elbow. He came upon me ascending the dusty road in the opposite direction, arguing with a farmer about "the shot that makes buffaloes give more milk."

The gatekeeper handed me what must have been a telex message read over the telephone from Rajdhani. It was trying to be in English, but both the reader and the receiver must have been Dhurgastani to have managed to so thoroughly garble it.

It did not actually matter very much really, the word "heart attack" was clear enough. The word leapt off of the bright page, grabbed me by the collar and slapped me across the face. I left the farmer without a word of explanation and started for home. I stopped en route several times to try to get more out of the message, but "heart attack" was all that I could manage; all else was a blur.

We had left the U.S. two years earlier, half expecting to never see my father again. He had already had one encounter with heart surgery and did not seem to have much of the terrier in him, just no fighting spirit. So every time I was unexpectedly called to some distant telephone (a blessedly rare occurrence in Dhurgastan), I wondered if this was the time. Was I about to wing around the world in order to see a casket laid into the hole in the carpet of astroturf? I had considered myself forewarned and prepared.

It is one of the heavy dues paid by every missionary with living parents. Now my moment had arrived, and I could not make my brain register whether or not he had survived the "heart attack." Joanne had to decode the message for me. It emphasized that the danger had already passed but that there was a need for surgery; that was about all that we could make it say. It left many questions unanswered and worries that the family was trying to spare us anxiety.

Dhurgastan, as far as the earth's rotation is concerned, is as distant from my parents' carport as any address on the planet—twelve hours' time difference. Whether one went east or west did not matter, the jet lag to muddle through was exactly the same. And so we had to wait long hours as the sun crept over the sky, waiting for the Western hemisphere to wake up before we could call. A few more hours were not important; the telex, probably considered so instant by my mother, had taken three days to reach us. By the time we called its message could be old, optimistic news.

The lines to Rajdhani were down that evening in any case, and we could not put a call through then—or the next evening, as it turned out. Tuesday night the phone crackled and hissed at me angrily, but I managed to yell the number to an operator with marginal English. He then sent my voice ricochetting off of a satellite all the way around this globe, which can at times seem so large and then in the next instant so small and parochial. So what if it took three days to call; who am I to complain when once in a while a miracle doesn't come through?

Things were already more stable at home. They had succeeded in persuading my father to have the surgery, and it was scheduled for the next day.

Besides letters, telexes and broken telephone calls there are other forms of communication available to the missionary today. Once there was a note in our mail slot from our Asia area director in Bangkok—another urgent request for information essential for budgeting, received by us on August third. "Please have it back to me August second; fax it, if necessary."

Joanne and I rolled our eyes. Then I asked her, "What does 'fax it' mean?" She shrugged, "Probably stands for something," she suggested. "Hmm . . . fast as . . . ," I tried. "Fast and expedient," Joanne said.

We had been away from the advances in mainstream technology for awhile and had never heard of the marriage of the photocopier and the telephone. I filled out the form and dropped it into the mailbag. "Fax," I said hopefully.

Cassette tapes—not sermons or music, but friends' voices, please!—were like ice water out in the endless, parched dunes, and about as readily available. And every blue moon or so, some thoughtful person would send us a photograph of the crew at a get-together; they had considered it so mundane that they had almost not bothered to document it on film. Just friends joking around a living room in Chappell Hill; it had not come out too well. Neda had an unpleasant expression on her face and everyone's eyes were glowing red from the flash. I can hear it now, "Ugh, this is terrible. . . . I know what! Let's send it to the missionaries."

But Joanne and I would be ecstatic and pore over it like scientists at the jet propulsion laboratories looking for evidence of volcanoes on dim and distant Neptune. In the corner . . . what was that patch of brown, was that an indication of the color of the new carpet on the Mays' floor? Was that only a shadow, or could we begin to see Leslie's pregnancy? Is that a new watch peeking out from under Willie's shirt sleeve? My, doesn't everyone look healthy and pudgy!

Reading over all of those Saturday afternoon letters from us kept by my parents brings the little weekly crises flooding back, but this time more in perspective. I can now see the big trends; some of them good, others sad and embarrassing. The early letters hurt just beneath the surface, stinging with homesickness; but they also pulsate with naive excitement and a spirituality glad of opportunity to roll up its sleeves. Slowly over time the eager confidence fades and they begin to complain and sound worn and unpleasant. The shiny dream of setting Asia alight with the gospel's fire tarnishes somewhat. That flame is never quenched completely, but harsh experience does what it can to close the damper.

But, despite the grumpy, self-absorbed tones at the end, there are some encouraging signs. Dhurgastani names are dropped more and more frequently—village friends are being made, neighbors turn into entertaining individuals rather than the initial bewildering mass of brown faces with black hair.

Village life must lose its sparkle; life must become mundane. No one could possibly continue to live in that initial whirlwind of emotion that we weathered. And this is a dangerous point of decision: what is going to take the place of that sparkle? We like to act as if it is not true, as if there is no such thing as a "failed" missionary. It is, I suppose, a spectrum, because all of us fail in some cases and to some extent. But as the sparkle dies, do we continue to represent Christ in a homey neighborliness, or do we instead turn inside, learn to make do in the climate, to carve out and insulate a homelife, not quite, but nearly, a replacement of that from our home country? Do we get creative in our recipes with the local spices available and find a new set of missionary friends—all at the cost of bolting the door to the society that we came to serve?

CHAPTER 14

The Beggars of Paradise

Missionaries and Financial Support

"He was penniless, he was parentless, he was to all appearances without a trade or a plan or a hope in the world; and as he went under the frosty trees, he burst suddenly into song."

G.K. Chesterton

Picture a ragged gray monsoon afternoon, wet clouds cut the tops off of the hills around our green valley. I walk home past puddles filled with smug buffalo that are enjoying a good wallow; my black cloth umbrella leaks in the center, and the rain runs down my elbow in a steady rivulet. My mood matches the weather.

A pig surprised me at the farm and died of some myoneuropathy which I could not fathom, though I was not lacking advice; all of the farm staff and most of the village population had stopped by my office to offer their diagnosis and to advise me as to its treatment. Also our concrete fish pond turned out to have a crack in it. We had constructed the small rectangular pond as a place to cure ceiling tiles, and it had held water then. Now that we have stocked it with three kinds of carp it leaks at an alarming rate. We can keep it full with rain run-off from the farm roofs collected by an ingenious system of bamboo gutters that Dhananjaya made, but in the dry season we will have big trouble keeping the fish submerged.

The village's electricity is off and so on this rainy day the interior of our house is dark. I leave my soggy shoes and socks at the door; everyone else wears sandals this time of year but for some reason I cannot seem to acquire the habit. After nine years of marriage Joanne can tell how I am feeling by the way I walk across the green in front of the house, and she meets me with a much-needed mug of coffee and conducts me nurse-like to my cane chair on the second floor to convalesce. Sitting there under a wool blanket I can look out over the water-logged landscape and open the mail.

Amid the envelopes is a thick packet of supporter cards sent to us from the home office of our Mission in Seattle. These are blank cards that are included with our monthly prayer letters; supporters are asked to write to us their thoughts and messages of encouragement on them. And they work on both counts: we delight in going through them and even acquaintances who could not manage a full-blown, self-initiated letter would jot down something and slip it in with their monthly donation to our efforts in Dhurgastan.

Somewhere along the line, however, it was policy or part of a tallying process to, in a very neat hand, write the amount of the accompanying check on the card with the message.

The cards were priceless; we needed assurance that we were not forgotten after the entry was dry in the checkbook register. But the figure in the corner was not precious. I tried not to notice them, not to see that Eunice had decreased her giving (but then, of course, John had lost his job at the hospital). I tried to read the messages and not glance at the amount; but my eyes kept going to it, not because they wanted to or because of an insatiable curiosity on my part, but just because it is the job of eyes to glance around unrestrained and take in all of the available information.

After reading a name and then seeing that they gave fifteen dollars, how was I supposed to feel? Appreciative . . . shocked at their unexpected generosity; . . . but too often—why that old cheapskate, and with all that filthy lucre, too!

My parents are firmly Republican, products of the Great Depression and are like the rest of their generation, better aware of the value of a dollar bill than spendthrift children. Good, down to earth, hard-working stock; and I was, therefore, raised with an understandable distrust of the welfare state foisted upon my people by conniving East Coast, Ivy League liberals. Were not the Scriptures clear in that pithy passage about "He who will not work, neither let him eat"?

I retain much of that early inculcated disdain of the massive, centralized, social bail-out, although I have been tempered by my experiences in the world's second poorest nation. But my precious Protestant work ethic suffered one gnawing inconsistency: as a missionary I worked among people who could afford neither my presence nor my technology. I was, in embarrassing fact, on the Church's dole.

Other missionaries, from more socialist countries and without my mythology of the self-made capitalist, rankled beneath the necessity of financial donations, too. All of us would have much preferred to simply charge the Dhurgastanis a fair price for our professional services. Only catch: the average annual per capita income in Dhurgastan is $146 U.S. We could not rely upon the free market to keep us working in Asia.

The problem of worthy causes

We are used to causes chasing after our tax-deductible money; the awful problem is choosing between the plethora of worthy ones. There is the opera, the alma mater, our own congregation, the new hospital expansion, the gubernatorial candidate who is going to save the state's educational system. Perhaps fund raising for missions work is understandable or easily forgiven by you; but for me it was a large, dead, soaking wet albatross hung around my neck. I fought many, awful, late night battles with the idea that I was a no-account, good-for-nuthin' shirker. And then, of course, TIME and NEWSWEEK had to reach us with scandals (sexual as well as financial) of the American "televangelists." I moaned as European brethren questioned me about it. Were we really any better than these greedy pseudoministers of God's good news?

Well, of course we were. But it is not unhealthy for missionaries to battle with the question periodically. Is what I am doing worthy of the trust that my supporters have placed in me? We cannot think strictly in terms of "souls for the buck"; nevertheless, am I being a good investment of the Church's resources?

And those resources are indeed limited. As a veterinarian with a nondenominational mission board, funds did not come automatically to me from some giant budget built from the dutiful tithes of congregations all over North America. I had, instead, two logical "constituencies": Christian veterinarians and small churches without their own mission agencies which yet wanted to be involved in work overseas.

The problem of deputation

Deputation is the word most often used by agencies for

the process of finding money for their personnel and projects—four syllables that jab a cold blade of fear into the heart of even the most toughened missions worker. "Bowel talk" or tales of horribly inconvenient travel are the usual conversation around a guesthouse dinner table in Rajdhani; but deputation stories kill the spirit of the evening, raise the blood pressure and send people to huddle in bed with the Agatha Christie novel which they had picked out from the library downstairs.

I had spent some bone-wearying time pounding the pavement in both parts of my constituency, a bitter process that erased from me any secret, cherished idea of having a political career. Saturday night I drove over to show my slides and speak to a home Bible study. It was a lively, charismatic group which I thought suspected me of being a closet church historian, an awful charge in their view because everything between the canonization of the book of Acts and about 1964 was obviously spiritual dead wood that needed burning in the blaze of God's Holy Spirit. The room was too warm, and they tried to squeeze me into the evening's program without cutting anything else from the usual routine. Before I was half through with my presentation I could see faces before me drawing the curtains, turning out the lights.

The next morning found me preaching at a crisply orthodox church with Gothic architecture and the opinion that any tradition not personally known to John Calvin was more than likely heresy needing to be burned in a blazing zeal for God's Word.

It was a tearing, stretching sensation, something like that experienced by the rope in a tractor pull. Both congregations decided to support our work in Dhurgastan, but I had the definite impression that those pledges would have been hastily withdrawn had either church known that I had had dealings with the other.

The Mission sent me to the Western States Veterinary Conference, a colossal event with thousands of veterinarians and hundreds of exhibitions held in Las Vegas. Visiting Las Vegas was a fascinating and yet nauseating experience for me. One day's "take" at some of the larger casinos would be enough to fund all of the Christian work in Dhurgastan for an entire year.

I manned a small booth in a corner of the giant display area. The response was inspiring as vets stood in a line to speak with me about ways to put their professional life at the service of God. But again the diesel engines growled into life and began churning in opposite directions:

> **First Man in Line:** "Hello, I'm practicing in Lincoln, Wisconsin, and just wanted to drop by and shake your hand and say what a great job I think that you guys are doing."
>
> **Martin:** "Well, thank you very much. You've heard of our organization before?"
>
> **First Man:** "Oh, sure. I've been a believer in the Lord Jesus for nigh on fourteen years now . . . got saved out of the Lutheran Church. Thank God. You know, a person can't go to heaven if they really follow all of that stuff the Lutheran's have added to the Bible. . . . Well, keep up the good work!"
>
> **Martin:** "Thank you, we'll try. Be sure to take one of our newsletters if you're interested . . ."
>
> **Second Man in Line:** "Hello, I'm Vincent Spence from Iowa. Saw your sign here and thought I'd drop by to let you know that I'm behind you fellas, and to tell you to keep it up."

Martin: "Well, thank you very much. You've heard of our organization before?"
Second Man: "Oh, sure. You had a representative come by our church, that's Sacred Heart Lutheran in Jefferson, and I can't tell you how excited it got us all about spreading the Word of God around the world."
Martin: "I'm very glad to hear it. Please be sure to take one of our newsletters . . ."

Eight hours a day for three days—I would rather be the sparring partner of some big boxer with forearms the size of my thighs, even if he was in a particularly ugly mood. It left me gasping for air and despondent at making sense of the Church in America. Where along this endlessly exclusive spectrum lies God's truth? Where is one to plant one's flag?

Painting an accurate picture

The awful thing was that the person speaking to me (Mennonite, Quaker, Baptist—Conservative or Southern—Wesleyan, Dispensationalist, premillennial, postmillennial or amillennial) considered me his trusted ally. If I was "okay," then I must agree with him, right?

The cynical answer is "money is green no matter who it belongs to," but Christ does not need any cynical representatives. The problem is that too many people are already using questionable means to raise money for laudatory ends.

In all my time in Dhurgastan I only saw one child about to die from malnutrition. His mother brought him into a mission hospital as an "emergency." And of course he was, without strength to raise his large head with the sunken temples and the huge, disproportionately bloated belly full of ascites. The German doctor was tired and yelled at the woman that this was no emergency; this child had been ill for weeks and they had brought him in just in time to die on his hands.

My friend was being harsh but not cruel. The parents had to be shown their responsibility for the neglect, otherwise the tiny child had no chance of surviving. He was going to die unless he spent three weeks in the hospital, and he might die in any case.

The parents looked at each other—three weeks; this was impossible! Someone would have to stay with the child the whole time, and they could not afford to do without the help of even one pair of hands in the fields this month because it was time to harvest the rice. (In Dhurgastan hospitals there must be a family member present to help with the nursing of a patient. Hospital staffs cannot provide all of the labor necessary.)

The point is that when people fund-raise for my support or for that of my project, they should not do so as if I am dealing on a day-to-day basis with starving children (an appeal statistically proven to open hesitant American wallets). I have friends who work in refugee camps in Ethiopia for whom that is an accurate image, but it was not so for me. I certainly saw hordes of undernourished kids, and most definitely my role as a teacher did increase the calories available to a family in the form of meat and milk; but no, I was not on a front-line position in the war on hunger.

The temptation is to present all urgent work as if it were vital and life-and-death in order to gain the resources necessary to get the needed job done. But this raises the stakes too high, callouses our compassion and inflates emotional appeal until no one is moved to help anyone unless things are already critical. If even then. Charles Colson (a former aide to President Nixon) said, "Power can corrupt us in Christian service as easily as it can corrupt those in political service." When asked what were the three most important ingredients in Christian work, Colson replied, "That's easy. Integrity, integrity, integrity."

The temptation to misinterpret the need, the work and our accomplishments is great . . . and subtle. No one in resource acquisition intends on being dishonest. The greatest service that we can render is to be cool and correct in telling the Church of its task. Certainly the staggering statistics are on our side with billions of Asians who have never heard about the love of the God who is really there; and, despite millions of dollars in aid over the past four decades, the agricultural output of Dhurgastan has actually dropped in each of the past five years. Our attempts to help are valid; they are just being out stripped by the deteriorating situation. Things are getting worse faster than they are getting better. As we try to express these facts to the Church and our society, we must educate them, not pander to their thirst for the sensational.

We compete for the limited humanitarian, or even more limited Christian, dollars. Give to orphanages in Calcutta! No, make that check out for irrigation for Somalia! Evangelize Cambodia as its Buddhist doors creak open! Me, me! No, me!

No wonder decent people who meant to help, throw their hands over their ears and go back to playing Nintendo.

No wonder the relief agencies turn up the volume, find ever and ever more shocking photographs to put in their advertisements in *Audobon* magazine.

The fieldworkers are above it all most of the time— hoping that the home office is being honest, wishing that they had more funds with which to work. More money would not mean wealthy missionaries; it would mean more work done.

Putting it in practical terms

In the hills of Dhurgastan there is a rabies problem. This is probably the worst disease that I encounter; it can be so hard to diagnose at first, and it is a hopeless cause once symptoms begin. No one has ever recovered from an infection. Our first day in veterinary school they showed us an old black and white film of a little twelve-year-old boy dying of rabies. It insured that we never forgot to take it seriously and that we would all troop obediently over to the health center that afternoon to receive our vaccinations.

People continue to die of it in Dhurgastan, but the mission hospitals carry neither the preventative vaccine nor the post-exposure treatment. Why?

Not because of any lack of concern, but because of a cold, calculated policy. With restricted resources, they do the best they can. For the price of one post-exposure treatment for rabies, the hospital can vaccinate dozens against tuberculosis, a much more common scourge to the population. They make the decision knowing that it dooms a few people a year to a terrifying death, but it saves many from a lingering one.

It is the kind of decision which is removed (to some extent) from Western hospitals because of our wealth; we can treat both diseases. It is the kind of decision that digs at a compassionate mission doctor, especially when that first person with rabies is carried through the door into his or her crowded ward.

CHAPTER 15

Dropped behind Enemy Lines

The Idea of "Spiritual Warfare"

"For the devil, though he has lost the sanctity, retains the sagacity of an angel, and is wise to do evil."

Matthew Henry

Dear Folks,

Saturday was crazy and trampled over my usual letter writing time, but I shall try to get something on paper this afternoon.

Church yesterday lasted several long hours—a young Dhurgastani friend was speaking before the congregation for the first time and let the time get away. That's interesting; when I'm nervous I speak too quickly and my talk is finished too soon. Once when I spoke at the village church, the congregation would not believe that I had let them out early until I actually rose and went out the door myself. Part was nerves and part was restricted language. My vocabulary keeps me from getting verbose.

Henk came over after church for coffee and a meeting that he had called at our place. Our church's Indian pastor and the headmaster of the boarding school were invited over to discuss the problem that we have been having at the farm with ghosts.

Put in that bold way it sounds silly, but were I to phrase it "strange occult occurrences," it might make a more serious impression upon you as you read this in the predictable, sunny, three-car garage comfort of an American suburb.

Henk has been wrestling with the problem for five years, whereas I am a relative newcomer. Let me give you a pertinent character sketch of my boss: absolutely no one could be further from a superstitious ninny than this statistically minded, give-me-only-the-facts kind of a Dutchman. To describe him as a nervous ditherer given to groundless hysteria would be to mistake a fully loaded moving van for a tricycle. If Henk gave credence to the frightened tales being told by the farm workers, then I would be stupid to laugh lightly and dismiss them. And recently he was concerned enough to take what action occurred to him and wrote for the advice of a missionary who lives in Pakistan and is famous for handling cases that involve demons.

When he told me of this step I was mildly surprised, but last week academic interest sharpened its teeth and became real involvement when he told me that our expert was vacationing in Bhadrapur and would be coming by our house after church.

Tell me, what image comes to the forefront when I say "a woman who has gained a large reputation after thirty years of dealing with evil spirits"?

Whatever odd person rose to mind, I should imagine that she had little in common with our real visitor who arrived at the door on the back of Henk's geriatric motorcycle. She looked like the pictures of P.D. James that I've seen: a matronly British grandmother, dignified but not austere, approachable but not a gadfly, with features that would defy the memory of a bank teller. Thankfully, her manner was similarly reassuring. No wild, romantic gesticulations. No Transylvanian lisp, nothing in the slightest flighty or hinting at a hunger for the sensational. Merely a charming English woman blinking intelligently behind her rather large, but not too large, eyeglasses.

She began her side of the conversation with a disarming introduction. She knew only too well that many Western Christians are uncomfortable discussing the undeniably supernatural; they consider themselves beyond the primitive notion of demons, and she made clear that these are what one actually confronts when dealing with legitimate "ghosts." She said that she understood this discomfort because for her first eight years overseas her own theology had not had room for real time, real space, fallen angels. She did, in fact, speak to most of my misgivings. I am orthodox in theory, but was rattled by encountering all of this off of the page of Holy Writ and in my own living room. It all sounded too blasted New Testament.

She spoke to the pastor about the need of educating the local believers—not out of their fears, but *past* them. It isn't that wicked spirits do not exist in fact; it is that we have triumphed over their powers through the Messiah. She also recommended that special services of prayer should be held at the church and at the farm. The service at the farm should include a group of believers walking around its perimeter the whole time, praying and "reclaiming" the grounds by the blood of Jesus Christ.

Very heavy, also very complicated. You see, not all of the expatriot team is happy with the idea, and the farm land is actually leased from the government. Ooh, what a fuss would be kicked up were the district governor to hear of such Christian goings-on.

In the end, nothing was done at the farm about our "spirit problem," probably because of the fear of stepping on the sensibilities of our superstitious Hindus or those of the rationalistic Westerners.

It is all too much like waking up to find yourself on page fifty-two of a Stephen King thriller. The reason that the village allowed the Mission to build on this land in the first place was because they considered it troubled. It is down near the river where they used to burn dead corpses. Lots of dissatisfied spirits were said to roam about it. The Dhurgastani employees are, of course, aware of this notoriety. And they are also aware of the tale of a past night watchman at the farm. He claimed to be bothered by a ghost one night while on duty. No one paid him any attention, and he died on the farm within a week.

The replacement was observed by a missionary to go into a "trance" one night and to shake uncontrollably.

The stories abound. Uneducated, Hindu imaginations can weave some pretty frightening tapestries from such material. This society is filled with a dark religion, rife with gory divinities that render even grown men afraid to go out after dark, especially near a river after the sun sets, for it is up and down these that the ghosts are thought to wander in search of the unwary. Such an environment "primes" people to imagine horrible things.

Though I can see that scary stories told around spluttering cookfires have no doubt magnified things, I cannot discount that there is something original around which the elaborations have been added. Our Lord Jesus certainly took these things seriously—much to the embarrassment of liberal theologians. Was He merely an uneducated man, steeped in His own era and "primed" to believe in anthropomorphic devils? Was He only playing games with His own contemporaries by ascribing to Satan what He knew to be epilepsy and lithium deficiencies? Or did His followers later doctor the gospels in order to give them more zing?

Your son,
Martin

More than scary ghost stories

The missionaries told their own stories, but usually under electric lights rather than spluttering cookfires, and they were usually a more subtle hue though recognizably of the same color.

Bupta, out in barren Western Dhurgastan, had the worst history for being a "dark place." That was the description soon to surface in any disquisition on the project; but what was meant by it?

Different things to different people. It was a land in which the entire population seemed to view thievery as normal human behavior. If you were so foolish as to lose and I so crafty as to make off with your possessions, then you did not deserve to own them, and I did. It was a place in which the sexual morals made the rest of Dhurgastan cringe, an area where the gospel could not seem to take root and grow and spread into a healthy, indigenous church.

It was also a difficult posting for the missionaries. No one thrived; they only survived. They broke out in boils or had marital problems; some were sent out depressed or suicidal.

But why was it a "dark place"? Did Satan hold more sway over a particular piece of real estate?

I was sent to Bupta to look at the agriculture department of the technical school there. I went out aware of the reputation but completely unsure of what to expect.

The stories were accurate about the local people. They went about forever unbathed, dressed in dusty black rags and would not engage in friendly small talk like the warm Dhurgastanis that I had met elsewhere. They even considered immigrants from Rajdhani to be suspicious foreigners, and the Mission had great trouble keeping the project staffed with a language instructor. Some of the stories were also true of the missionaries. Living conditions were not as rigorous as I had envisioned, but the staff there was tired, discouraged and prone to bickering with one another and about one another to an understanding outsider like me.

The team spoke a lot of spiritual warfare; in fact, that had been the topic of the project's Bible study for the past nine months.

Bupta was a "dark place" where all was so saturated in demon worship that spiritual weapons were needed to blast a beachhead for the Church. The team needed to be on its toes, but I also sensed that the team had begun to see a devil beneath every stone—and Bupta was a rocky place. As C.S. Lewis so correctly observed, Christians can make two mistakes when it comes to Satan: one is to ignore him or consider the adversary an unneeded antiquity; the other is to dwell upon his wiles for too long. After nine, slogging months it was past time for the study to be upon the joy of the Lord. That, after all, is said to be our strength.

My own experience

I am a veterinarian, a "dog doctor" as a friend at our church in Austin insisted on calling me to prevent me from taking myself too seriously. Yet we are as steeped in experimental science as any discipline. If you approach me with a new pharmaceutical said to be hot stuff against a specific condition, then you had better be armed with figures about its indications, contraindications, pharmacokinetics and mechanism of action as well as unassailable evidence of its efficacy. During the years of training we became dour and critical, and in practice we have witnessed enough sure-fire victories go astray that we gain a working pessimism.

I maintain, therefore, that I am about as unlikely a candidate to rush willy-nilly into tales of spiritual adventure as my boss Henk with his head as hard as his wooden shoes. I cannot help it, nor do I think that I would help it if I could.

As a Christian I stand convinced of the existence of unseen powers that can produce palpable occurrences, and yet the powers themselves remain at one step's distance. Our machines cannot quantify them; they do not trigger the automatic doors down at the grocery store. But being a Christian and standing so convinced does not license me to bulldoze over the intellectual equipment which God has provided. We are to be discerning. The startling line which I read and came slowly to agree with was that "our first moral duty is to think properly." I have had friends who "rebuked Satan" every time they forgot and locked their keys in the car or dropped their checkbook into a mud puddle. I knew a dear woman, completely normal to this layman's eye, who told me that she met a demon at a formal dance once. The creature was dashing and humanoid in its tuxedo until she glanced down and noticed its large, yellow, rooster feet protruding from the cuffs of its well-tailored trousers. What can I say? I was not there, and yet I doubt her. It seems unlikely.

I am aware of the insult to our college-educated sensibilities presented by the idea of spiritual warfare. But battling the unseen forces means more then dealing with goblins and rattling chains. I believe that a missionary is much more apt to meet the conflict in unsensational forms: that petty bureaucrat who is so unaccountably uncooperative, that inexplicable "thing" that comes between you and your office mate, the crippling doubt that assaults you during devotions. These are just as real as, and quite possibly more dangerous than, the trees that rustle down by the farm when there is no night wind, or that silent man dressed all in white that appeared by Gopal's father's funeral pyre and then vanished.

The Vietnamese defeated both France and the United States because they avoided pitched battles, which would have given their mightier adversaries the advantage, but maintained instead a constant guerrilla pressure that wore out the energy and willpower of their enemies. It would similarly be of little strategic sense for God's enemies to draw up against us in open warfare. In such a situation our fear would send us immediately into the very camp from which they hoped to sever us.

Nevertheless, odd things happen, and missionaries usually have some queer experiences to tell. I have only three of these, and none of them is real headline quality. At the time events always went too quickly for me to see the big picture, though I was aware of a door seeming to open in our familiar dimension that allowed me a moment's peek into something else.

The first happened to me early in my time in Dhurgastan, when I was more impressionable. It was during language school and we were all out on the time known as "village stay": three weeks away from the crowded capital, out in the country to catch the rhythm of the rural culture and to try to catch as much of its Basha as possible. Joanne had to return to Rajdhani after the second week. She was pregnant with our first son, and the meals provided by our village family were not enough to satisfy her growing needs. Therefore I was left to finish the time alone in my little loft next to the house.

Since that village stay I have cherished a small soft spot in my heart for the monkeys taken out of their lush jungles and put on display at a city zoo. My life was one constant attraction. Early (oh, so early!) in the morning, when my eyelids made their first tentative flicker of the day, excited whispers could be heard at the door at the bottom of the ladder where some watchman looking through the crack could inform the rest of the eager audience that the exhibit was awake. And that was just the first moment of a day lived in this same vein, with all of the immodest situations which come to the reader's imagination: how did you ever manage to . . . where could you . . .? Exactly. And thus must feel the monkeys. Remember this the next time you visit the primate house with your children and are disappointed because the Purple-Collared Gibbons refuse to play entertainingly.

Late one night in my cozy loft I awoke with a start, immediately alert. I could not have made out the face of my watch, could I have found it, in the inky interior. Only one blue slash of moon ripped across the foot of my bed through the shuttered window. I can only try to describe the sensation that seemed as if it filled the tiny room. I was not conscious of having dreamed as one usually is if startled awake by a nightmare; but I was filled with a great, black dread. No, that was not it. The blackness, the dread, was outside me, but pressing in from all sides. I was frightened, not as if by a boogie man, but as if the man-eater that I had been hunting by day was now sniffing around the flaps of my tent by night. This, however, is too descriptive without being informative. It was a crushing intuition that something malevolent was with me in the darkness. I have never felt anything like it before or since; I had always shook my head unsympathetically when people described a sensation of evil that seemed to cling to a Hindu shrine. Ordinarily were I to awake in such a state, I would assume that I had heard in my sleep the snap of a twig or the creak of a board beneath the foot of a flesh and blood intruder; but I was instantly quite sure that this was something else, something which required prayer instead of my flashlight.

It was only several moments later that I began to hear a small sound that rose and fell on the wind. Voices were chanting to the clack clack of something like sticks being beaten together in a rapid rhythm. These were men and women, I think, not too far away, but distant enough that the noise would never have roused me from my sleep.

I got up the next morning to the usual gratifying audience; but the sun did nothing to diminish my conviction that, whatever it was I had encountered in the night, it had been real. Only later did I put together that it had occurred on a full moon, a time of special ceremonies out in the hills.

My second apprehension also happened in a rural situation, but two years later when I was more jaded and more difficult to surprise. Again it was suddenly upon me with no presentiment or building anxiety. It happened sandwiched between perfectly mundane events.

We were in the busy midst of our vaccination campaign against hemorrhagic septicemia, and Som Prasad and I, with a group of two or three others, were going up a stony trail to some houses perched up in a wet, windy pass. Gray clouds flew through a notch in the hills like smoke through a keyhole.

Just as we topped the last bit of ascending trail we found ourselves in a lovely setting sheltered from the raw weather. It was a courtyard formed by three substantial village houses and roofed by the boughs of an enormous banyan tree. A beautiful spot, not at all sinister or given to morbid thoughts. A small knot of locals stood on the red clay of the courtyard and watched us approach with subdued interest; a man and a woman squatted on the near house's veranda.

Before I had taken in my surroundings fully, it was suddenly as if some internal watchdog had leapt to its paws inside of me and was quivering with excitement. Not afraid, but on guard. And I was just as suddenly aware that I did not like the man who was squatting on the porch, though he was perfectly innocuous so far as my reason could tell. At the same instant he seemed to become animated with a hatred for me, because a fierce, glaring, diabolical expression broke across his face; but he continued what he was doing which only now did I have time to notice. He was murmuring very quietly, almost inaudibly, and apparently the same things over and over again. Then he would purse his lips, never taking his eyes off of mine, and blow into the face of the woman who squatted next to him with her eyes closed. Next he would take the tail feather of some bird and brush at the woman as if dusting off a piece of furniture; then he would go back to his murmuring. All the while he stared knives and daggers at me; no fear on his part either, but rather as if sizing up an opponent before entering the ring.

I have never had such an expression leveled at me, and I really did expect him to jump from the veranda and be upon me all teeth and claws. As I prepared for the attack (because you don't look at people like that unless you mean to attack), an insistent thought demanded my attention: if the man comes at me do not swing at him with the walking stick, but exorcise him.

I could tell that I meant it, too. Right there in the latter part of the twentieth century.

"But I've never seen an exorcism, nor do I have any desire to!" I was aware that I "heard" a second voice; and I recognized in it the normal Martin, the one who was not used to encountering crazy situations. This one wasn't commanding; as a matter of fact, it sounded kind of jittery. It complained that it couldn't exorcise anyone; it didn't know any of the proper protocol or formulas.

That's okay. If he heads your way, you give it to him but good. Make it loud enough for everyone to hear; no formula required, just be sure to do it in the name of the Lord Jesus Christ.

No one was more relieved than I that the witch doctor (for so I later learned him to be) did not make that fatal move. I am not sure that I would have possessed the guts to be very authoritative about the whole thing. And what if the demon had only chuckled at me? Worse yet, what if nothing at all had happened? What would the others have thought then?

Using authority

The third incident, as usual, came in low and hard before my sonar had time to register its approach. I was in no sense primed and out prowling for a whammy experience; I go out of my way to miss such experiences, I'm afraid. No, I was sweating away under a heavy shirt and inside the extremely "this-worldly" setting of a crowded Dhurgastani bus. I was en route back to Bhadrapur, bringing with me one medical and two veterinary students who were in the country for six weeks trying to see mission's work from the inside.

The bus was stopped for an unknown reason, and, deprived of the wind made by its motion, the interior became steamy and filled with cigarette smoke. A beggar boarded at the door toward the back and began his way up the aisle; nothing out of the ordinary about the scene in the slightest.

But this fellow was erratic. I could see him coming, but pretended not to, as one learns to handle this type of situation. He begged from no one until he was next to me, and I tensed. Here it comes; put the bite on the white "tourist." However, I was left unmolested, and instead he targeted a typical-looking farmer in the seat in front of me.

The beggar was a young man, hard to age but not too far from twenty in either direction. He had the scant, scraggly beard of neglected youth, ugly protruding teeth and a vacant look to his eyes. He knelt down in the filthy aisle, bending all of the way over until his forehead nearly rested on the bus' floor. Then he began to move a cupped hand rapidly back and forth between his head and the feet of the man in front. The beggar never looked up even to see if he was being noticed, nor made any of the pitiful murmurings of the professional beggars. He just kept the hand going back and forth with autistic-like concentration.

The Dhurgastani farmer got embarrassed and tried to send the boy on his way, but there was no response. Then to lift the beggar away from his feet; at which, with frightful suddenness, the boy made an animal-like noise of fury and frustration and tried to bite the farmer's hand. As quickly as it had happened he was back to his silent supplications at the shocked farmer's feet. I had never seen an outburst quite like it, nor, obviously, had the hapless victim; disturbing the process brought such a frightful retaliation.

The watchdog was again at its station, warning that this was no normal situation. I argued with it that this was surely a great human tragedy in front of me, but no more. This poor boy was mentally unbalanced, and his voice had seemed like that of a deaf person who had never had the benefit of speech therapy. This behavior was merely an awesome ploy developed to extort compliance from his would-be benefactors.

The farmer had meanwhile marshalled his forces and had taken as much of the game as he would. He began beating the boy about the back of his exposed head and shoulders, and this started a great snarling and snapping and cursing that sounded exactly like the tussles I have engaged in the runs behind a veterinary clinic. Once the farmer really committed himself, the skinny boy had to give way, and he retreated toward the front of the bus, only to collapse at the feet of a new person and begin the horrible process all over again.

The bus' population began making ominous noises, and I began to pray. Didn't the Lord realize that I could not risk doing something melodramatic in front of all these witnesses?

Why not?

Well . . . well, I might end up looking a fool. Or being a fool, I don't know. Just don't ask me to get involved, it isn't fair. It's not my business.

Another fight had broken out in the aisle, and in the melee the beggar got pushed into my medical student. There was a look of abject terror on her face, and I thought that the poor girl might try to jump out of the window. The entire bus was alarmed now and on its feet. Several men were going forward in a determined manner, and I could tell that the young boy was about to get beaten to a pulp.

Demoniac or only retarded, something had to be done; and I found myself on my feet and cutting off the attackers who were still behind me in the aisle.

"Stop it," I said in a commanding voice.

The bus was silent instantly, from my tone or because the foreigner knew Basha or just because an odd situation had ascended to new heights of weirdness, I do not know. The boy looked at me with his vacant eyes. "Follow me," I said and walked past him and out of the door at the front of the bus as if he had no option but to obey. Even as I walked out exuding such confidence, I believe that the normal Martin was afraid that the beggar would not comply.

But he did, and meekly, without a word.

We were facing each other out under the hot sun and with every face in the bus pressed to a window watching us. The cornered animal had left him, and he was completely passive. I was too unsure of myself to make this an out-and-out exorcism. I was not sure that was called for, although a large part of me suspected it. I was even too frightened to touch him; the idea of a human bite has always been disgusting to me. My performance, I suppose, was pathetic: I merely told him firmly that what he was doing was wrong and that he was not to do it any more. He was to leave . . . instantly.

I then turned my back to him, half expecting to feel his teeth at the back of my neck, and climbed back aboard the hushed bus.

The beggar boy left without a whisper and disappeared into the bustle of the roadside village.

What should one conclude?

I have listed here three examples, back to back, and it leaves one with the impression that I am sensitive, perhaps too sensitive, to such occurrences—maybe that I was even out gunning for them. I protest that I was not. These three brief experiences, however, were scattered throughout three long years that were brimming with exotic happenings and even more full of slow, unremarkable days when existence seemed to drip by monotonously.

Actually I probably do not hunger for spiritual experience in the healthy way that should be quite natural and proper to a loving follower of a supernatural God. Good friends have told me that my faith is too calculating and cerebral. Miraculously answered prayers, more often than not leave me feeling frightened and disquieted, instead of grateful and happy. I'll just believe in You, God; but don't You do anything. It scares me when You do things. And so, with such an attitude, it is natural that blatant, unadulterated, no-holds-barred spiritual warfare usually feels far removed and kind of unsavory to me.

CHAPTER 16

Wonderful Complications

Marriage and Children Overseas

"Now it happens that this Candaules was in love with his own wife; and not only so, but thought her the fairest woman in the whole world. This fancy had strange consequences."

Herodotus

I was given a piece of sound advice: Always insure that pressures are kept to your outside shoulder and are not allowed to come between you and your spouse. In this way, as the pressure builds, instead of forcing the two of you apart, it acts to drive you closer together in loving reliance.

It's a lovely image that's aesthetically satisfying. But it leaves two simple questions unanswered: a. What does it mean? b. How is it to be implemented practically in a day-by-day, real-life situation? As a picture it was picturesque; as sound advice it was moot.

Life in Asia was an atmosphere of unforeseen pressures in which we walked and breathed and worked for three years. How does one keep all of that to one's "outside shoulder"?

January 25

Mom and Dad Lewis cut the apron strings today. Much to

my abject terror. We took a solo taxi ride to Prem Sadan Guesthouse—a lovely place: sunny garden with a little fish pond in which golden carp lounge in the afternoon. We have a very airy room that opens out onto this garden—the least depressing place to my tastes that we've stayed in yet. It will be a pity to leave it in less than a week and move in with our Dhurgastani family. This p.m. Joanne and I were finally alone after three weeks in Asia, finally a chance to find out how the other was coping. Walked to the Blue Star Hotel for dinner. Realized that I've been unfair to her. Scared myself, I resent having to feel responsible for her as well; also I have a tendency to accentuate her weaknesses and fears and thereby in some morbid, twisted way make myself appear to be adjusting better than I actually am. It is a diabolical, unnatural competition. None of this has been conscious (I hope), but I think it is how I've been operating. Must stop it, and instead cultivate a sense of humor and perspective. Might as well make the most of the situation and go through it all the best of friends. . . .

March 30
. . . I've not been treating J. well at all. I give everyone else my reserves of courtesy and attention, leaving her only surly tidbits. The guilt is worse because at present she needs me more than ever.

April 18
. . . spent the night alone at the education office's "escape room"—a place they've reserved for language students who are living in local homes, as somewhere to go when it all gets to be too much. A monthly day of solitude, silence and evaluation might be rejuvenating—but this one bore me no particular fruit. I could barely pray or even think, but

managed to read a little of the Scriptures. Today the Syme's had a little daughter—Mel and I went by to visit—a precious moment (that occurs by the billions). Joanne and I did get to have a good talk about us this evening—so perhaps the night away wasn't a waste. I pray we may improve—I must be more patient and sympathetic. Our worlds have drifted apart under the constant barrage until J. has no real idea of all that has been happening in my thoughts recently.

Is counseling needed?

When we returned to America three years later we were "debriefed" by our sending agency in Seattle. In our file was a letter from the personnel department in Dhurgastan that stated that, though we were wanted back after our furlough, it was felt that it would be good for us to undergo some marriage counseling.

We were shocked at this revelation, not because we had not survived some hard knocks as a couple, but because in our experience, all missionary marriages rub spots raw while overseas. The people in Seattle were embarrassed to have to make the recommendation; they were unaware of where or by whom it had originated.

Joanne and I racked our collective brains over the incident, trying to think of where such an ominous letter might have come from. We suggested various conversations, and then began to see a trend. Both of us could remember times at various fellowship groups where it was advocated that as a group we share more intimately in order that we might be of more immediate and vital support to one another. Joanne and I both took such invitations seriously and spoke of tensions that we faced around our household. Rather than the group continuing in a similar vein around the circle, each addressing the real, behind-closed-doors kind of issues and concerns, each time the group broke into heartfelt intercessory prayer on our behalf, and then everybody went home.

It was not unlike some junior high pact for everyone at the party to take their clothes off in the dark, only to discover when the lights came back on, that you were the only one of your friends to take the challenge quite seriously.

And reckoning that all marriages could do with some good advice, just how were we to approach a counselor? Hello. We're Joanne and Martin St. Kilda. Our problem? Well, while living in Dhurgastan under the most difficult conditions, we found that we experienced some difficult conditions. What advice do you have for us; you see, whenever we're under tension we feel tense?

Pregnancy on the field

Because a pregnancy might hurry a recurrence of Joanne's Hodgkin's disease, the doctors warned us not to have children for at least five years. Plus, they added, do not expect to ever have children—the chemotherapy that she underwent had more than likely made her infertile. We are both the youngest children of small families and, therefore, completely ignorant of "things baby"; but not being confident that one wants children is a very different thing indeed from having some emotionally detached health professional announce that the decision had been taken out of your hands by the same awful treatments that had spared your wife's life.

God was very kind to us, and our first son was known as "the miracle baby" around the Mission. Living in Asia seems to cure ninety percent of fertility problems, and this accounts for one out of four humans being Chinese as well as for the eight hundred million Indians, not to even mention the populations of Thailand, Vietnam, Myanmar, Malaysia. . . . Mankind may inhabit the earth, but he lives in Asia. And it was now our turn to do our part; after eight long, quiet years our comfortable marriage woke up to find itself expecting.

Joanne was pregnant within two months of our arrival in Dhurgastan, and this kicked over a can of paint that colored all of her experiences during the time there. As strange new combinations of hormones surged and ebbed, as her petite anatomy performed aerobatics that we would have before considered impossible, she was unable (and forever shall remain unable) to decide which of her feelings were produced by Dhurgastan and which by her endocrine system.

We would awake in our tiny room up on the third floor, and our stirring would send the rats muttering back up the walls to where they slept during the day. The pungent odor of rice and curried vegetables being cooked over kerosene would waft their way up the rickety ladder from Bijou's kitchen. I rose hungry, but Joanne did not seem able to join in my enthusiasm over breakfast; and her appetite, never huge, faded away into a shadow of its former self. How must our hostess feel when Joanne's steaming plate was left untouched? And this became one of those times when Martin the hyper-missionary guarded the feelings of others at the expense of his wife's. "Make yourself eat," came my helpful exhortation, which might as well have been, "Here, bite into this live jellyfish!"

In Dhurgastan (we later learned), it is unthinkably crude to discuss one's pregnancy with anyone. This is based on several things: it might invite catastrophe from some unfriendly and meddling spirit; and, of course, the idea quite naturally brings with it thought upon immodest topics. Pregnancy, and those events leading to and following from it, are all quite natural and certainly take place frequently in Dhurgastani home-life, but they are never to be discussed, not even between husband and wife. Why, it would be as if I were to refer to . . . but no, I can't even write about such things!

But we needed to explain the situation to Bijou who giggled at our confession (goodness, do these weird foreigners have no decency?); as a mother of two, she understood. She told us that when she was . . . that way . . . she had had to cover her nose and mouth with her sari as she stirred away over her cooking pots in the morning.

Pregnancy also had another odd effect upon Joanne, seeming to bump her gyroscope just a fraction out of alignment. Perhaps it was her changing center of gravity, maybe the want of appetizing food, but she lost her usual grace and became an uncoordinated klutz. In America, so slight a loss of coordination might go easily unnoticed, but in Dhurgastan it was a dangerous liability that manifested itself daily. Bicycling over rainy, muddy streets through the maniacal traffic of Rajdhani is an exercise requiring the nerves, reflexes and finesse of an accomplished trapeze artist. And all this was asked of a pregnant woman pedaling uphill in a crowded city that does without any control of its sewage. The gutters along some of the streets we used were full of a black ooze that bubbled slowly; and you might recall that our route to the language school led us past the city dump, a place that after three days of heavy rain cannot be experienced by proxy. One has to do it one's self. Cresting the top of the never-ending hill brings no relief. It brings instead the wild, headlong rush of descent: dodging taxi doors that are suddenly flung open, weaving between un-predictable pedestrians, threading the needle through a dog fight that spills off the sidewalk and into one's lane.

Outside of the condensed muck of the city, out in the countryside, things are not actually much better; one mere-ly exchanges a certain kind of obstacle course for another. There are walls to be clambered over, walls that are lined with stinging nettle that is quick to reward a false step with a sensation like that of sticking a bobby pin into a wall socket. There are jiggly ladders to be negotiated up into dusty sleeping lofts. Walking along the dikes between rice paddies, Martin the hyper-missionary is trying to be cool because the village is watching, when behind him . . . splash! She's done it again. . . .

October 31—All Hallow's Eve
9:15 p.m. Salyan House

And so my whole life is changing this evening. Joanne has just gone to bed aided by 10 mg. Valium, p.o., and Kerry White (an Australian nurse with the Mission) is on a mattress in the corner. Contractions are still mild—but they have definitely begun. The past months have gotten me excited about the prospect of having a family. I think back upon the few good ones that I have experienced as an outside observer: the Presslers, the Pardues, the Raben-horsts. What do these all share in common? Each are Christian—where Jesus is important to both father and mother, lots of *love* for the children is evident, other people also get included freely—there is lots of activity. And so now Joanne and I are beginning. It is very hard to believe. *Oh God, help us in this undertaking; help us to do it all as unto You—the wonderful as well as the painful. And Father of lights, aid and teach me to be a father like You: Wise in his dealings. Responsible in his care. Firm in his discipline. Strong in his support. Diligent in his own ways and always in pointing toward You as the ultimate source of all good gifts.*

Today Joanne and I have two sons: one born in the primitive inconveniences of Rajdhani, the other, in the modern inconveniences of Houston's Medical Center. The two very different experiences leave me strangely quiet— neither a frantic advocate of natural childbirth, La Leche League or Lamaze, nor a worshiper at the altar of invasive medical technology if its greatest motive is to prevent litigation over negligence. We have seen both ends of this particular spectrum and have found each to suffer their own peculiar absurdities.

Ethan St. Kilda was born on November first, into a city too distracted to notice his advent coming as it did on the last day of the meetings between the eight-member nations of the South Asian Association for Regional Cooperation. The streets of Rajdhani fluttered with the flags of Bangladesh, Bhutan, India, the Maldives, Nepal, Pakistan, Sri Lanka and Dhurgastan. The traffic policemen wore pressed uniforms and faultless posture. The streets were all but closed as scores of motorcycle outriders escorted end-less heads of state and foreign ministers in their black limousines displaying their own fluttering flags over the front bumpers. All very high level and aggravating:

"You can't go that way. Outta the way!"
"But Officer, my wife is having a baby!"
"Get on; that's an old one. Now beat it—the Grey Poupon of Rajneeshi is on his way!"

We managed to argue our way to the hospital, and my first sight as we hit the front door was a quaint one which we would not have had back home. An ancient Tibetan monk in his maroon and gold robes was on his way out, his long scraggly beard looked like Spanish moss growing from the chin of his wind-parched face. He placed both palms together and nodded reverentially, assuming that I must be a mission doctor. Inside a second sight greeted us; this one was not quite as quaint but just as unlikely—a dirty, little girl, of about eleven years old, with her filthy dress hiked up around her waist, was urinating under the stairs.

Dhurgastani culture and religion are very definite and do not shilly-shally with our western confusion over the division between men's work and women's work. Having babies, to their old fashioned way of thinking, falls very clearly to the latter, and Dhurgastani husbands are to have even less to do with it than Victorian ones used to. The wives like it that way; they do not want menfolk present either. Both sexes consider it a mortifying situation—just this side of shameful, and religiously, it is definitely defiling.

I was not, therefore, as welcomed as I might have been at a modern Family Birthing Experience Center; the Dhurgastani staff only tolerated my presence because I was a missionary, and they could therefore not be sure but that I might be someone important in the hospital's budgeting process.

Joanne did it all without even an aspirin—not so much because of a theology which required birth pangs, nor an aversion to epidurals; it had more to do with it being a harsh necessity. I spent the last few moments out in the hallway at the obstetrician's behest, and when that wee meow-like complaint first reached my ears something awesome happened.

Mount Palimar National Astronomical Observatory

Internal Memorandum: Colleagues, please note that at 13:01 g.m.t. on 11/1/87 the earth was measured as having "reeled" upon its axis. Seeing, however, that no long-term or untoward effects of the incident have been as yet verified, and in the absence of any suitable scientific explanation of the phenomenon, this institution has officially chosen to ignore the occurrence. Please remember this in your dealings with personnel associated with the media.

The Director

Yes, things were "primitive," and if young Ethan had required an incubator all that would have been available to him was an old cardboard box once filled with Druk Fancy Fruit Jam and a sixty-watt light bulb. A doctor friend of mine in Texas had taken me aside at a farewell party for us and had advised me very forcefully, "Don't be having your babies over there." (It is interesting that the United States is a dismal nineteenth best in infant survival rates.)

The problem of protecting your children

We were aware that having children in a Third World nation largely devoid of recent advances in technology was suboptimal. To be frank, we knew that if Ethan had contracted the streptococcus infection and stopped breathing his first night like one of his friends in America had, that chances were excellent that he would have died. And this brings us full-face with that oft-mentioned worry over children's health. "I cannot serve overseas, although I would like to, because of my children's health. It is one thing to risk my own life but a very different one to play Russian roulette with the lives of my kids."

Rather than hashing over the statistical realities or appealing to the doctrine of God's providence in order to calm these anxious parents, I think that it is best to agree with them. Yes, if your bottom line goal is to take absolutely every available precaution to minimize all physical danger to your children, then it is best to stay in a developed country. I cannot argue the point. We felt that we had better health care while in the Mission because so many of our good friends were physicians, but the truth was that there was a greater probability of our requiring their expertise than if we had been living in suburbia.

"Yeah, and what about their education, and . . . and their socialization process?" might ask the anxious parent, encouraged by my conceding to their first concern.

Ah well, this is another kettle of fish entirely, and I am not willing to give any ground here at all. I, in fact, believe the mission field to be a superior place to grow up in many ways.

We were in the guesthouse in Rajdhani when friends returned from a five-month furlough in the United States. I assumed that they needed especially tender care at first; it was bound to be a difficult time for them as they settled back into the maddening routine after having once again tasted the old, familiar luxuries. But not a bit of it—they straightened me out on this point as soon as we began talking. They both proclaimed themselves to be relieved to be back in Dhurgastan, not because they dislike reliable electricity or were uncomfortable in a homogenous cultural setting in which they understood everything spoken to them; no, they were glad to be back for the sake of their children.

American society is youth crazed, but not in any well thought out, logical manner. Young Americans are itchy to grow up, eager to face the adult world of fast cars, expensive watches, sex and chemical abuse. Ironically, simultaneously the rest of the population lusts for youth regained. Fourteen-year-olds determine the nation's tastes in food, television, music and fashions; everyone else trips over themselves to imitate them and make a buck in the process. Neither the little ones nor the big ones can decide on the optimum age, but it is certainly over twelve and under thirty-one.

A kindergarten teacher from New Zealand once told me that she found MKs who were home with their parents on furlough to be a delightful breeze of fresh air. She said that they possessed bright, active imaginations in comparison to the lifeless, listless apathy of their peers. MKs may be deprived of the glut of new diversions that keep children inside watching a screen, but any reflection will find them wealthier for their poverty.

And as far as education goes, I will happily pit a remote project's tutorial group to mortal combat against a well-equipped and prestigious private school in the home culture. The MKs will have read more and read more deeply; they will have picked up one or maybe two new languages, and they will be more colorblind than children bussed across town in hopes of legislating away segregation. Simply by virtue of the fact that they live in a culture not native to their parents, MKs grow up in an atmosphere heavy with the adventure of learning. They benefit from closer supervision by their teachers. Miss Ann, who teaches them in the morning, is the same young Irish woman with whom they go camping on holidays and worship with on Saturdays.

Recently thirty percent of graduating high school seniors in America were unable to find the USA on an unmarked globe. What chance do they then have of understanding the viewpoints, politics and histories of other nations? That is a sort of functional illiteracy which never occurs on the mission field.

Before deciding whether they are properly socialized you had better define your terms. Plenty of MKs ride skateboards (on the rare patch of smooth asphalt), but if you mean are they on the cutting edge of the latest pop culture fad, then I suppose they may be six months (perish the thought) behind in what weirdness they perform on their coiffure. If, however, you mean have they learned to share and help and work with others different from themselves, I'll let you decide.

Isn't missionary life monastic, a little Christian hothouse existence where your child only knows believing adults that have only one limited viewpoint? Yes, all of the Finnish and Dutch and German and English and Welsh adults that Ethan knew were Christians, but most of the Dhurgastanis were Hindu. How many Buddhists does the average American eight year old know? Who then is it that is poorly socialized?

I was busy in Dhurgastan with animals, employees, sickness, church, colleagues; but I had more time with Ethan there than if I had been in a mid-sized veterinary practice back home doing emergency duty every other night and every other weekend. It's true that I missed his first birthday party (a crazy mixture of village and missionary children) because it was the day we found the embezzling going on at the clinic, but I could walk home for lunch everyday.

CHAPTER 17

That Fellow Who Came In with You

Missionaries: How They Change and How They Don't

"Wherever you go, there you are."
Buckaroo Banzai

God is not dead, but poor Zeus certainly is. Except for tourists and sheep, Mount Olympus lies deserted. The Hellenic gods and goddesses are extinct; their myths have fallen from being serious theology into neglected literature. Mankind, however, continues unable to live without myth; debunk one and another crops up in its stead. Modern men believe in *change*.

We have learned from the scientists, from Copernicus and Keppler and Galileo, that what is obvious and common knowledge today is tomorrow's childish ignorance. Ask any eight-year-old which it is that is actually moving, the sun or the earth, and see if it is not so. We have arrived at the usual place where we expect all things to change; we expect for all that we know to be true to be disproven—if not in our lifetime, then in that of our children. We, as modern man, believe in progress. The past has nothing to teach us; our hope lies in the future.

Our problem comes when we get confused and believe

235

that all change is progress. Saying that labels me a dinosaur and a Luddite, but life does not work that way. The choices confronting us are real choices; it is possible for us to take a wrong turn. This is as true for a missionary as it is for an astronomer or a taxi driver.

Living overseas will bring changes in one's outlook and character. It does not necessarily bring progress. One's horizons are broadened; it can't be helped. Twelve thousand miles' distance, foreign colleagues and Hindu neighbors all bring a new perspective to one's home and all of its cherished certainties. I learned about British politics and why it is that Margaret Thatcher is more popular in the U.S. than she has ever been on her island home. I heard about German education, about the wisdom of providing technical training for the many and an academic training for the few; about the Swedes and how thirty percent of them take adult education classes purely for self-improvement, how Dutch prisons function, why Australians disdain Marmite but crave Vegemite—and how the English do exactly the opposite.

I had a remarkable discussion with a brilliant young Dhurgastani on the subject of marriage. To begin with, I looked down my aquiline, Anglo-European nose upon the local custom of arranged marriage as being primitive and unenlightened. In its place I propounded the wonders of love-marriage (my friend referred to it as "lust-marriage"). He was eloquent, persuasive and (alas!) armed with statistics about the state of American marriage. By the end of our argument, had I been honest, I should have conceded myself bested. Perhaps I will not try to arrange Ethan's marriage, and maybe I cannot convince Western society to leave its hedonistic ways, but I do here admit that the old, Oriental method (the method throughout all of Bible history, I might add) sounds best. Overseas, along with the microbes, one is exposed to a lot of new opinions; not everyone votes Republican . . . or Democratic, for that matter.

These experiences and ideas and strange people come along as if upon a conveyor belt set to go one enthusiastic notch too quickly. One is asked to react, to decide, to assimilate; and before one unfamiliar situation is resolved, there is another one in your lap. Is it immoral to use DDT in the starving Third World? Can you sponsor me to go and study in your country? What is a Hindu convert to do with his second wife? Shall we teach the use of steroids in our farmer courses if they are available in the bazaar? Do I pay this outrageous Dhurgastani income tax on all of my income or just on what I bring into the country? Does it make any difference that all of the other aid organizations are tax exempt? Should a non-Christian national with the most seniority be made a Section In-charge in the Mission? Can I have money for medicine for my baby? Why is it that you say "God bless you" whenever I sneeze? May I use your bicycle? Oops, here's your broken bicycle back. Is it wrong to drink alcohol? Then why did Jesus do it? Aren't Catholics just like Buddhists? Why did your country invade Panama and yet argues with the Soviets about Afghanistan? Can I borrow your wife's bicycle? Oops . . .

The bombardment goes on and on, never letting up, never letting you crawl out of the bunker to collect the wounded and identify the dead. You do react. You must decide. You will change.

But the changes are real choices, even though they may go by like telephone poles as you speed along the highway. You wake up one morning and realize that it has happened. Things once hard for you about life overseas are now routine. Naiveté gets replaced with wisdom; but naiveté can be lost along with one's vision and ideals. One gets used to seeing poverty, used to it and either remains compassionate or grows cynical. Friction can produce muscles, but it can also cause callouses. Senior missionaries are all toughened—some shine with hard-earned love; others glow with the cold fire of a grumpy disenchantment.

Change and improvement

Our missionary checks in at the ticket counter two hours early for the overseas flight, sees to it that all of the trunks get labeled and pays the overweight fees, sits around the waiting room not knowing what to say to gathered friends and family, boards the airplane (the hostesses are wearing saris!), kills long hours flipping through the airline magazine (the duty-free gifts seem to belong now to another world), watches at the window as the green hills of Mimbwebwe materialize through the low lying clouds and then (surprise!) . . . emerges from the airplane exactly the same person, minus several hours sleep, as the one who boarded it.

Actually, there is no surprise in this; we all know that travel does not bring automatic character improvement. If it did family vacations would be more popular. It does broaden one's horizons, but take that trip in the car out to Eunice's in Arizona. It broadened horizons all right (that state has miles and miles in which one's only desire is to hurry and get to the horizon); but, what with the kids being in such a state the whole time, it cannot be said to have brought you much in the way of sanctification. Why should it be any different for the missionary? Travel is forty percent anxiety, thirty percent traveler's checks, twenty-five percent slide film, four percent disappointment and whatever is left is for enjoyment.

People will say, "I don't know what made me do that. I was under stress, and it was most unlike me, really." Stress can bring out some awful reactions: a bursting flash of anger, a whining self-pity, a latent cruelty. But stress, like hypnosis, cannot bring out of us anything that was not already there. When all is calm and sunny, we wear a suit of social respectability; let things get stormy and we shall see the flesh beneath.

If a person is wracked by some besetting sin (and honestly, who isn't?)—some gnarled, ugly thing inside that we struggle to keep a secret—or if, on the other hand, he has that one hulking flaw about which everyone knows, he must not go overseas hoping that the new surroundings will correct the problem. Be it ever so well-guarded a secret or stamped in blue ink under your bangs and across your forehead, that detestable "thing" will stay at your heels on the journey. Missions is not the chase scene in a detective movie; we cannot "lose them" by going far and fast and pulling "tricky ones" at busy intersections. Nor is missions a dramatic get-away like the French Foreign Legion (which I hear isn't so dramatic itself).

Do not become a missionary to escape a temptation or to overcome the ravages of a broken heart. Do not go in an effort to prove something to those friends who do not take you seriously. Worst perhaps of all is going in hopes of gaining God's admiration:

> I do not want to go to Africa as a missionary because it is the worst thing that I can think of, but we all know that God wants us to do the worst thing that we can think of, and we should be willing to do anything for God, and so I'm going to Africa.

Don't laugh too hard, it happens; and everyone pays the price.

CHAPTER 18

Check the Heat Shields for Reentry

Returning Home

"Dogs look up to us, cats look down on us, and pigs treat us as equals."

Winston Churchill

The last month in the village was just as if we had died and yet been made executor of our own estate. Everyone had been coming for weeks—just to chat—and as they rose to go, "By the way, what are you going to be doing with that pressure cooker? Are you planning to take it home?" The vultures were gathering overhead, but the carcass had not stopped twitching yet. Everyone wanted to tell us how much we meant to them, what a fine contribution we had made, to plead with us to come back after furlough . . . and to stake out their claims as to our household belongings.

After three years of simple living, we had amassed quite a fortune: the Sanyo stove, our water filter, six coffee mugs, a few plastic buckets. And now the Saracens rode down upon us to plunder. The raiders were missionaries as well as Dhurgastanis. No offense, no harm in it; we'd done the same to other departing friends—where do you think I got that snazzy typewriter?

I am an abject weakling and would send people away with armloads of used objects, but Joanne would catch them at the door. No, put them back. Everyone must wait for the big sale like everybody else. Nothing was going for free. It wasn't good for people to give them things for free; if you gave to those who asked, it only meant that the noisy and the greedy got ahead.

The great day dawned, and I made sure that I stayed down at the farm all day long. Joanne was made of firmer stuff than I and could watch our lives in Dhurgastan be picked through. And it was like a group of sharks during a feeding frenzy, an ugly, repellent sight. It did have its moments— Raju, a very modest young man, managed somehow to buy a maternity bathing suit in the melee. He came back the next day to return it, extremely embarrassed and holding it as if it were a dead catfish.

The church of course wanted to send us off and recognize our efforts in the congregation. We knew the routine, and I also knew my enormous hat size. To prevent embarrassment I had bought a topi (a Dhurgastani hat that looks like a soft, brightly colored flower pot) months earlier in Rajdhani. I had to purchase it in the capital because my seven and one half size was so rare. I then wore it everyday, to the village's delight, so that everyone knew I had one and that it was unnecessary to buy me one for our farewell.

Saturday, after the sermon, the pastor called us to the front of the packed room. We were made to sit there as friends came by and draped strings of flowers around our necks. Then the youth group came forward and presented me with the obligatory topi. They were astonished when the size five flower pot perched on my head like a dunce cap. Sigh. So much for the plans of men.

The old pastor then eulogized us, speaking of how hard

we had worked and how very dependable we had proven during our year there in the village. There were nervous coughs around the room. A friend spoke up and corrected him—"They have been here for a full three years!" Thank you.

But it was okay. Symbolic in a way of a lot. Missionaries cannot afford to lose their sense of humor or to take themselves too seriously. The village has seen plenty of bright, eager faces come and go; and as far as our sacrifices—well, they had always lived this way. One cannot expect gratitude or one will get sour. A friend once put it well when he observed, "You can tell if you have a servant's heart when others begin to treat you like a servant."

It is hard to leave one's new culture, the Mission, the work. And it is downright murder to leave all of those dear friends. But that is also okay. You would not want it to be painless. What would it say if it was easy to leave, if your desire to go was not mixed with a large portion of real sorrow?

The reverse flight

And so you board the airplane once more, only this time it is with a familiar destination awaiting you at the other end. But is it really so familiar?

Ironically, at the last instant the empty seat beside me was filled by the same fellow who had been the first person that I met in Dhurgastan: Dave, the language coordinator, the one who had taken me over to see our room at Bijou's . . . oh, a lifetime ago at least. He was going back to the U.S. after twelve years in Asia. He would be coming back after a year, but not to Dhurgastan; his mission needed a teacher in India.

The plane taxied down to the end of the runway, and we

spoke of all the emotions churning away inside. Unfortunately, I couldn't help hearing a woman in the seat behind us talking in a high-pitched whine, "Why she never did anything about her facial hair, I'll never know. All that she would have to . . ."

Thankfully the engines roared into life, and I could not hear any more. Dave and I sank into thought as the orange houses began to streak by the window faster and faster; we tilted back and then punched a hole in the clouds over Rajdhani. I couldn't see, but I'm sure that the hole closed behind us.

The reverse culture shock

We came back in time for the last minutes of the pre-Christmas rush, a feeding frenzy in its own right. Teenage Mutant Ninja Turtles happened to be "the" thing that year.

We were changed but in a way that only friends who had been overseas for extended periods of time could understand. People wanted to know. "So, what was it like? Did you enjoy it?" Presented with a plate heaping with turkey and ham, two kinds of dressing, potatoes au gratin, salad with mandarin oranges, three-bean salad and broccoli with Hollandaise sauce, my neighbor turned and asked, "Now, did you have anything like this over there?" I was so stupefied by the feast in front of me that I stammered, "Well, let's see. . . . We had potatoes." I'm sure the woman thought that I was either retarded or else trying to impress her with how hard my life had been.

Good friends are afraid of you when you come back. They don't know what to say and are in fear that you are now Jeremiah the prophet come to convict them of the sin of buying a riding lawnmower instead of giving all of the money away to the poor.

Family is glad that you "have that burr out from under

your saddle" and speak as if you have seen the error of your ways. They have no idea, much less sympathy, about how you grieve over leaving Dhurgastan, how you get teary-eyed every time Ethan asks to go back to his house and play with Nickolas, that rascally five-year-old from Melbourne.

The church has you labeled and nods as you speak, knowing beforehand what you will have to share, even though they may not be hearing a word that you speak.

You have become an amphibian; not quite a reptile and certainly not a fish. You don't fit in on the land or in the water, no longer a normal American and never able to be a Dhurgastani. People find you distressing and a little too pedantic when you take the wrong side of every argument that touches upon internationalism; you see Japan's side in the trade war and have become tolerant of unorthodox theology. . . . Why, of course we (whoever we happens to be) have a fuller, more correct picture of how God is working in the world.

So you learn to keep your mouth closed. No one with any sense appoints himself or herself to the office of prophet. It is cold and lonely up there on the mountain.

It isn't that you don't soak up the culture, however. It is unspeakable bliss to walk down a street and not attract a crowd of curious followers, to be able to understand every nuance of a conversation, to eat Mexican food and drink water straight out of the tap. You are surprised, and a little dismayed, with yourself at how easy it is to fit back into mindless television after dinner, to being too busy to sit outside and talk with neighbors, to speak of God as if He is a Protestant of English descent.

The worries of overseas are now exchanged for those of the future: What shall I do? Where shall we go? What shall we do for bread and clothes?

How we see each other

The trend these days is for missionaries on deputation, while speaking to a crowd, to use the line that "we are all missionaries." I have used it myself. And it is, of course, in some senses quite correct; but neither the audience nor the missionary believes it fully.

The missionary looks out over the people and thinks, "Poor dears. Ignorant as turtles about the world at large. They are only concerned about their own little pond." And the people are thinking, "Poor old rumpled thing. He isn't current any longer. He's going to be a misfit from now on." And again, of course, in some sense they are all quite correct. But I have come to see that the call of God quite routinely means being called to be a misfit.

> You are My witnesses, says the Lord, and My servant whom I have chosen, that you may know Me, believe Me and remain steadfast to Me, and understand that I am He. Before Me there was no God formed, neither shall there be after Me. I, even I, am the Lord, and besides Me there is no Savior. (Isaiah 43:10-11, The Amplified Bible)

EPILOGUE

A Note for Prospective Missionaries

Men and women of various ages and in different circumstances quite often wrote to me and asked what things they might do in order to prepare themselves for foreign service. This book would not be complete without at least a brief word addressed to this.

In one sense, those things that one should do to prepare for serving God in a foreign culture are exactly the same as those one should do to serve Him in the home culture. In other words, do not tire of being faithful in the obvious.

There do remain a few, specialized suggestions:

1. Put yourself into cross-cultural situations before you take the large step of leaving your homeland. If you are white, get to know some blacks or Hispanics or ask that Vietnamese fellow who works at the corner store over for dinner. If you're black, get to know some whites. . . . You see the point; put yourself in contact with people different from yourself and learn how you react. Foreign students at a nearby college are always hungry for new friends.

2. Minister among the poor. If you are open to the idea, there are plenty of opportunities. Let your pastor know that you would like to work with your

church's mercy ministry, or get in contact with a church in your community that has such a thrust.

3. Begin living more simply. Learn how you get along without every material convenience. Our experience was more like camping than anything else, and we also saw that it was more difficult in general for affluent Americans to adjust than any other group of missionaries. But everyone must settle for themselves, without peer pressure, what constitutes simple living. Husbands especially need to be understanding of the needs of their wives.

4. Educate yourself to the world and missions. Most of the media does a terribly superficial job of covering world events. Subscribe to a good news magazine— I recommend *The Economist* from Great Britain (do not let the title put you off; it is not mostly financial news). Also read about missions: see *God's Foreign Policy* by Dr. Miriam Adeney. And read the biographies of famous missionaries: try *Amy Carmichael: Her Life and Legacy* or anything by Elisabeth Elliot.

5. Most importantly and most obviously, give priority to growing in your knowledge of God. Devote yourself to prayer, the communion of the saints and reading of the Scriptures.